10 INDIAN LANGUAGES
AND
HOW THEY CAME TO BE

KARTHIK VENKATESH

An imprint of Penguin Random House

DUCKBILL BOOKS

USA | Canada | UK | Ireland | Australia
New Zealand | India | South Africa | China | Singapore

Duckbill Books is part of the Penguin Random House group of companies
whose addresses can be found at global.penguinrandomhouse.com

Published by Penguin Random House India Pvt. Ltd
4th Floor, Capital Tower 1, MG Road,
Gurugram 122 002, Haryana, India

Penguin
Random House
India

First published in Duckbill Books by
Penguin Random House India 2024

Text copyright © Karthik Venkatesh 2024

Karthik Venkatesh asserts the moral right to be
identified as the author of this work.

ISBN 9780143461968

Typeset in Sitka by DiTech Publishing Services Pvt. Ltd

Printed at Repro India Limited

www.penguin.co.in

10
INDIAN
LANGUAGES

AND HOW THEY
CAME TO BE

KARTHIK VENKATESH

Read more in the 10s series

10 Indian Animals You May Never Again See in the Wild
by Ranjit Lal

10 Indian Monarchs Whose Amazing Stories You May Not Know
by Devika Rangachari

10 Indian Women Who Were the First to Do What They Did
by Shruthi Rao

10 Indian Champions Who Are Fighting to Save the Planet
by Bijal Vachharajani and Radha Rangarajan

10 Indian Heroes Who Help People Live with Dignity
by Somak Ghoshal

10 Indian Art Mysteries That Have Never Been Solved
by Mamta Nainy

10 Indian Tribes and the Unique Lives They Lead
by Nidhi Dugar Kundalia

Scan QR code to access the
Penguin Random House India website

To Sonu, my everything

10

10 INDO-ARYAN LANGUAGES

INTRODUCTION

HOW MANY 'INDIAN' LANGUAGES ARE THERE?

The number of languages spoken in India is much discussed and even more disputed. Many have attempted to compute the exact figure. What we can say with authority is that it is a very large number.

Among the earliest who attempted to count were the poets—Amir Khusrau in the courts of the Delhi Sultanate and Abul Fazl in Akbar's court. Writing in CE 1317, Khusrau listed Sindhi, Dogri, Kannada, Telugu, Gujarati, Tamil, Bangla and 'Hindavi' as the 'languages of Hind'. More than two centuries later, Abul Fazl in his *Ain-i-Akbari* (late sixteenth century) recorded most of these languages and added Pashto, Marathi, Lahnda (Punjabi), Marwari, Baloch and Kashmiri to the list.

These lists are far from comprehensive but this is what these poets knew of, sitting in Delhi. Nonetheless, they establish the point that the Indian subcontinent was home to many languages, an observation that many foreign travellers also made over the next few centuries. But the actual number of languages was to remain a mystery for much longer.

British administrator Sir George Abraham Grierson undertook a 'systematic survey of the languages of India', which started in 1894. This was the Linguistic Survey of India (LSI). The LSI was published over a twenty-five-year period (1903–28) and consists of eleven volumes (in nineteen parts) of descriptions of the languages and dialects of most of British India (some parts of southern India were not surveyed). For the first time, Grierson actually came up with a number that had been comprehensively researched. The LSI listed 179 languages and 544 'dialects'—a total of 723 distinct tongues.

Each of the entries in the LSI was accompanied by what Grierson termed 'specimens'. In the initial volumes, a standard passage was translated into every language. Later, a second specimen, a piece of folklore or another story of some sort in prose or verse was added. The listings in the final volumes were also accompanied by a list of words and sentences. For the final few volumes, audio recordings of various people speaking the language were also made.

The 1951 Census of India listed 784 languages. The 1961 Census of India listed a total of 1,652 'mother tongues', later pared down to 1,100 languages. The 2001 and 2011 censuses both listed 122 'major' languages—languages with more than 10,000 speakers. Since 2013, the People's Linguistic Survey of India (PLSI), spearheaded by G.N. Devy, has recorded the existence of 780 languages and estimates that there are about seventy or eighty more, which they could not record.

Given these estimates over the years, it would not be incorrect to say that India is home to something like a thousand languages, give or take a hundred or two.

LANGUAGE AND DIALECT

One word that always comes up in any discussion about language is 'dialect'. What is a 'dialect', exactly? How is it different from 'language'?

In popular usage, a dialect is viewed as something of a 'lesser' language. When we speak of a dialect, we sometimes mean a language that is spoken only (without a script) and sometimes, a tongue that resembles a known language (say, Bangla or Tamil), but also has special features of its own—certain words, accents, sentence constructions and so on—that make it different from the known language.

In reality, language and dialect are ambiguous terms. Grierson in his introduction to the LSI compared it to 'mountain' and 'hill', two other terms that have no clear distinction between them.

The Hindi saying '*Kos kos par badle paani, chaar kos par vaani, par ek hai jo nahi badalta vo hai Hindustani*' (the quality of water changes every three kilometres, and the language after every twelve kilometres, but the Indian does not change) captures the situation succinctly. Scholars have proved beyond doubt that spoken languages demonstrably change every few kilometres or so, with speakers adding their own local flavour to it.

There is no language that is unchanged over a wide geographical area (*chaar kos par vaani*). That being the case, all languages are 'dialects' and vice-versa.

This distinction between language and dialect assumed importance only when large-scale printing became possible and texts in various languages became a possibility. In the late eighteenth century, large-scale printing in India began.[1] The need then arose to have a 'standard' written language that everyone could understand. Languages were then codified or standardized by developing dictionaries and spelling forms. In time, a new literature that was written in this standard form evolved. When people talk of language 'purity', they are most often talking about the 'standard' or 'model' language, something that they believe that all users of the language must aspire to achieve. People also mistakenly think that the standard version of the language is superior. But that is not so. It is just a matter of chance that one form of the language became the standard. There is nothing inherently 'superior' about it. The standard language is just one of the 'dialects' that got promoted randomly or due to external circumstances. In an alternate universe, another dialect could have become the standard.

LANGUAGE FAMILIES

Despite the many languages that exist in India, there are many features that many of these hundreds of Indian languages share at the level of sounds, words, sentences and speech patterns (. . . *par ek hai jo nahi badalta vo hai Hindustani*).

---

[1] The first printing press of India was set up in 1556 at St. Paul's College, Goa. But for the next two centuries, printing in India did not become very popular. The first Indian-owned printing press was established in Calcutta in 1780. Soon, printing became popular and in the nineteenth century, spread throughout the country.

India constitutes a distinct linguistic area,[2] and linguists classify the Indian linguistic area with its many languages into five families:

1. Indo-Aryan language family
2. Dravidian language family
3. Austro-Asiatic language family
4. Sino-Tibetan language family
5. The Andamanese language family

In terms of numbers, the Indo-Aryan family is the largest of the Indian language families. About seventy-five per cent of India's population speak a language belonging to this family and its speakers are also the majority in Pakistan, Nepal, Bangladesh and Sri Lanka. There are more than 200 Indo-Aryan languages. Some like Hindi-Urdu, Marathi, Bangla, Gujarati and Punjabi have tens of millions of speakers.

TEN MOST SPOKEN LANGUAGES IN THE WORLD (AS A FIRST OR SECOND LANGUAGE)[3]

English: 1.452 billion speakers

Chinese: 1.2 billion speakers

Hindi: 602 million speakers

Spanish: 559 million speakers

[2] A linguistic area is a space (a region, countries, or in this case, a subcontinent) in which languages from different families have influenced each other significantly, leading to resemblances across language family boundaries.
[3] *Source:* https://www.babbel.com/en/magazine/the-10-most-spoken-languages-in-the-world

> **Arabic:** 274 million speakers
> **French:** 274 million speakers
> **Bengali/Bangla:** 273 million speakers
> **Portuguese:** 258 million speakers
> **Urdu:** 231 million speakers

It is broadly accepted that all *modern Indo-Aryan languages* trace their origins back to Sanskrit. Sanskrit, specifically, the Sanskrit of the Vedas (hence Vedic Sanskrit), is the earliest Indo-Aryan language that is still with us. The Rig Veda has been dated to about 2000 BCE and is the earliest example of Vedic Sanskrit. Apart from Vedic Sanskrit, scholars also distinguish Classical Sanskrit, which is somewhat different from Vedic Sanskrit. Classical Sanskrit is the language of the earliest version of the Ramayana that is attributed to Valmiki (written around 500 BCE) and the earliest version of the Mahabharata attributed to Veda Vyasa (written between 400 and 200 BCE). It is also the language in which Kalidasa (who lived around the fourth or fifth-century CE) wrote his plays and poetry.

From Sanskrit, the road to modern Indo-Aryan languages meandered through two other destinations: Prakrit and Apabhramsa (pronounced Apabhransh). Prakrit is a term for a collection of tongues widely used from the fourth or fifth century BCE to the eighth century CE all over northern, eastern and western India as well as in parts of southern India. Linguists therefore do not speak of one 'Prakrit', preferring the term 'Prakrits' instead. These tongues spoken in the various regions then evolved into different kinds of Apabhramsa, before finally settling down around 1000-1100 CE as early forms of the various modern Indo-Aryan languages spoken today.

THE INDO-EUROPEAN LANGUAGE FAMILY

The Indo-European language family is the largest family of languages (by population) in the world. Close to three billion people (more than forty per cent of the world's population) speak an Indo-European tongue. The Indo-European language family consists of ten distinct branches—Anatolian, Indo-Iranian, Hellenic, Italic, Germanic, Armenian, Tocharian, Celtic, Balto-Slavic and Albanian.

The Indo-Iranian branch is the largest branch, with close to one billion speakers. It is sub-divided further into Indo-Aryan, Iranian and Nuristani. Languages like Hindi, Punjabi, Gujarati, Marathi, Bangla, Odia, Assamese and many others all belong to the Indo-Aryan group of languages. Pashto, Balochi, Persian (Farsi) and others belong to the Iranian group. The Nuristani group is an extremely small group consisting of languages like Kamkata-vari (40,000 speakers), Askunu (40,000 speakers), Tregami (3,500 speakers) and a few others which totally add up to a little more than 100,000 speakers.

Other language families in the world

There are 142 language families in the world. The five largest language families in the world are[4]:

1. **Indo-European:** 4 billion speakers, 448 languages (English, German, Hindi, Persian etc.)

2. **Sino-Tibetan:** 1.4 billion speakers, 457 languages (Chinese, Burmese, Tibetan etc.)

[4] *Source:* 'What are the largest language families?' https://www.ethnologue.com/insights/largest-families/

3. **Niger-Congo:** 600 million speakers, 1,539 languages
   (The languages of West and Central Africa)

4. **Afro-Asiatic:** 600 million speakers, 377 languages
   (Arabic, Amharic, Hebrew, Somali etc.)

5. **Austronesian:** 327 million speakers, 1,227 languages
   (The languages of the Polynesian and Melanesian Islands
   mostly)

Interestingly, the Trans-New Guinea family of languages (largely
found in Papua New Guinea and some neighbouring islands)
consists of 476 languages, but only four million speakers.

Besides the Indo-Aryan family of languages, the other
numerically significant linguistic family in India is the
Dravidian. By most estimates, Dravidian languages are
spoken by about twenty per cent of India's population.
Close to thirty Dravidian languages have been identified,
almost all of them in India. Today, Dravidian languages,
especially the four major languages of Tamil, Telugu,
Kannada and Malayalam, are the dominant tongues of
southern India. Tamil is also native to parts of Sri Lanka.
Pockets of Dravidian language speakers are also found
in central and eastern India. Kolami, spoken in Madhya
Pradesh, and Malto, spoken in Jharkhand, are both
Dravidian languages. Interestingly, a Dravidian language
(Brahui) is also spoken in Pakistan.

It is more or less agreed by most scholars that the early
forms of Dravidian languages evolved independently of
Sanskrit. Many are of the opinion, though, that speakers
of Sanskrit and Dravidian languages were in contact even
in Vedic times. The presence of Dravidian words in the Rig

Veda is cited as evidence of this. Some scholars claim that the language of the Indus Valley Civilization was a Dravidian one, but conclusive proof is lacking.

The Austro-Asiatic languages constitute another very important linguistic family. There are about 170 Austro-Asiatic languages found all over southeast Asia and eastern India. Worldwide, Khmer (Cambodia), Mon (Myanmar) and Vietnamese are three of the most widely spoken languages in this family.

In India, Khasi, Nicobarese (about six languages) and the Munda or Kolarian languages, the most important of which is Santali, are some of the widely spoken languages from this family. The Munda languages are spoken in Jharkhand, Chhattisgarh, Bihar, Odisha, West Bengal and in Bangladesh. The word 'kol' meant 'man' in many of these languages, which has now changed to 'hor' in Santali and Mundari. Some scholars believe that these languages might justifiably be called India's 'original' language group since there is some evidence to show that they probably predate both the Dravidian and Indo-Aryan language groups.

Santali today has more than seven million speakers. Mundari, another Kolarian language, has two million. The Khasi tongue, which is widely spoken in Meghalaya, has close to one and a half million. Till the nineteenth century, the Austro-Asiatic languages of India were only spoken tongues, lacking a written script.

The fourth family of Indian languages is the Sino-Tibetan (sometimes called Tibeto-Burman). The speakers of these languages can be found from Ladakh in the north to Arunachal Pradesh in the east. Meeteilon (Manipuri),

Ladakhi, Bodo (spoken in Assam), Kokborok (spoken in Tripura), Lepcha, Bhotia (both spoken in Sikkim), Mizo and Newari (spoken in Nepal) are the important languages of this family. The languages of Nagaland and many of the languages of Arunachal Pradesh also belong to this group. Owing to its extensive geographical spread and since many of the languages are spoken in remote areas with a very small number of speakers, the number of languages in this family found in India is difficult to state with certainty.

In Arunachal Pradesh, a unique experiment of sorts is underway. A script called the Tani Lipi was created at the beginning of the twenty-first century as a single script for the various tribal languages (twenty-six at last count). The creation of this script (by Tony Koyu) is essentially an attempt to record indigenous tribal knowledge.

A fifth family of languages has been identified and classified only recently—the Andamanese. Great Andamanese, Onge and Jarawa are the confirmed languages of this family. The Sentinelese language is believed to be a member too. But since the Sentinelese are an uncontacted tribe, this is hard to confirm.

The Andamanese languages belong to a different family from the Nicobarese which, as stated earlier, are all Austro-Asiatic languages.

Great Andamanese is a generic term used for ten closely related varieties of the same language once spoken throughout the Andaman Islands. The tribes of the Andaman have a history that dates back 70,000 years when the first migration of humans took place out of Africa. Till about three hundred years ago, the Great Andamanese tribes were spread all over the Andaman Islands, divided into ten different subtribes. Now all that is left is a mixed group of people of fifty members, who are descendants of different sub-groups. The Great Andamanese today are an endangered population of fifty, with only seven language speakers left.

Some scholars even speak of a sixth language family existing in India. This is the Tai-Kadai (sometimes known as Kra-Dai) language family, consisting of among others, Thai and Lao, the languages of Thailand and Laos. In India, a couple of languages spoken in Arunachal Pradesh and Assam are believed to belong to this family.

To better understand language families, scholars use a concept known as the 'Proto' language. A proto-language is an ancestral language from which other languages which are related to each other evolved over the course of time. There is usually no evidence of these proto-languages since they existed only in the spoken form. But on the basis of common words and other similarities across what are today different languages, scholars are able to reconstruct this proto-language. For instance, linguists believe that the ancestor of the Dravidian languages is Proto-Dravidian. Tamil, Telugu and Kannada evolved from Proto-Dravidian.[5] That explains why they are in the same language family.

In some cases, like the Austro-Asiatic language family, language families prove handy to try and reconstruct ancient migration routes. For instance, we know that Khasi, which is spoken in the Khasi Hills of Meghalaya, is related to the Khmer language of Cambodia. These languages are also

---

[5] In case you are wondering about Malayalam, as we will see later, Malayalam evolved from Tamil and not directly from Proto-Dravidian.

related to Vietnamese and a few languages in Myanmar. Given that many speakers of Austro-Asiatic languages are in southeast Asia and a few in the regions between southeast Asia and India, scholars conclude that the origins of this language family are in southeast Asia from where a group came further west, with some settling in Myanmar and some coming further to India.

LANGUAGES AND SCRIPTS

A script is a system evolved to record a language in a written form. But since the spoken language came much before the written language, the connection between the script and the language is not as strong as we perceive it to be.

A single language may be written in multiple scripts. For instance, Konkani is written in the Devanagari, Malayalam, Kannada, Roman and Arabic scripts. And all languages can (with some adjustments) be written in a single script. Text messages typed on mobile phones often use the Roman script for many Indian languages.

Also, knowing a script is not the same as knowing a language. German, French, Spanish, English, Kokborok and Khasi are all written in the Roman script. However, knowledge of the Roman script will serve no purpose in understanding these very different languages.

Sometimes, scholars also talk of situations where the same (or similar) languages are written in different scripts. In the Indian subcontinent, the best example of this is Punjabi, which is largely written in the Gurmukhi script (derived from Brahmi) in India and Shahmukhi script (similar to the Urdu script) in Pakistan. Yet another example is Hindi and Urdu. Today, Hindi and Urdu are considered separate languages though there is a lot of similarity between them. But that they are written in two different scripts isn't why they *should* be considered separate. They actually could be considered the same (or similar) language(s), despite their different scripts. In other parts of the world too, such situations exist. Serbian and Croatian are mutually intelligible, but Serbian is written in the Cyrillic script (also used to write Russian) while Croatian uses the Roman script.

Another important thing to remember about scripts is that for many centuries, languages were written in several scripts, sometimes in the same period of time. Often, there was no one agreed script for a language. Only with the advent of large-scale printing was it felt necessary to have one standard script for a language.

LANGUAGES UNDER BRITISH RULE

The British introduced English in India since it was the only language they knew. Their idea was that a small minority of Indians would be provided education in the language and would assist the British in the administration of India. Ironically, while many Indians did do so (though always a small minority), many more Indians after having learnt the language could now communicate with each other without a language barrier. English proved to be a great uniting factor during British rule, and this continues till today.

The Congress, which spearheaded the freedom struggle, used English extensively in its communications. But equally, the Congress also wanted to encourage the use of Indian languages. In 1920, it decided to organize its provincial branches not along the lines of the provinces as they existed under British administration, but along linguistic lines. The

Nehru Report of 1928, which envisaged the future shape of India after it secured independence from the British, made the commitment that provinces in a future independent India would be linguistically determined.

Another important development during British rule that enabled the growth and development of languages in India was the development of large-scale printing. Newspapers, magazines, books and all kinds of reading material became available in many languages and a strong linguistic consciousness developed.

MAHATMA GANDHI ON INDIAN LANGUAGES

In his work *Hind Swaraj* (1909), Gandhi articulated his idea of a linguistic order for India which consisted of what he called 'provincial languages' and a 'universal language', which in his view should be 'Hindi, with the option of writing it in Persian or Nagari characters'. English, in his view, could function as the language of international communication but was not suitable for India since most Indians did not know it. Though Gandhi advocated Hindi a great deal, at no point, did Gandhi endorse language imposition, but encouraged a slow and gradual acceptance for the pragmatic reason of having a national link language that would be entirely Indian. Equally, he also advised that Indians should learn more Indian languages to better communicate with each other. He recommended that north Indians should learn Tamil.

LANGUAGES AND THE INDIAN CONSTITUTION

The Indian Constitution attempted to deal with the language situation in India sensitively and even-handedly.

Among its most carefully considered decisions was the decision not to have a single 'national' language. English and Hindi are the 'official' languages of India. But besides these, the Eighth Schedule of the Indian Constitution lists twenty-two other languages, known as 'scheduled' languages. These are the languages that the government of India officially promotes. There were originally fourteen when the list was prepared in 1950. Eight more languages have been included since 1967 in response to the demands of different language groups.

LIST OF SCHEDULED LANGUAGES

1. Assamese	9. Konkani (added 1992)	15. Odia
2. Bengali/Bangla		16. Punjabi
3. Bodo (added 2003)	10. Malayalam	17. Sanskrit
4. Dogri (added 2003)	11. Manipuri (added 1992)	18. Santali (added 2003)
5. Gujarati		19. Sindhi (added 1967)
6. Hindi	12. Marathi	20. Tamil
7. Kannada	13. Maithili (added 2003)	21. Telugu
8. Kashmiri	14. Nepali (added 1992)	22. Urdu

Individual states are allowed to have their own list of official languages—those that are in the Eighth Schedule and also others that aren't. Kokborok, one of Tripura's official languages, is not a scheduled language. Khasi, which is an official language in some of Meghalaya's districts, is also not a scheduled language.

A wealth of linguistic richness exists outside the portals of state patronage as every state is home to several languages, besides the two or three official ones.

India, therefore, is not only home to many languages—
the languages of India also have long and varied histories.
During the many centuries that these languages have been
in use, the people who spoke these languages have had
contact with speakers of other languages. As is natural,
the languages then changed owing to these interactions
and due to the many uses that the languages were put
to. For instance, words and phrases were borrowed or
coined when literary works were written. Scientific works
demanded a separate vocabulary which either had to be
created or borrowed.

Languages, like human beings, are ever-changing. Just
as there is no such thing as a 'pure' human being, there is
no such thing as a 'pure' language either. Human beings
and languages just are.

While the Constitution makers did a commendable
job in handling the complicated language situation in
India amicably, the Congress government under Nehru
dragged its feet on creating linguistic states. Owing
to the large-scale violence that accompanied Indian
independence and Partition, many feared that further
divisions of the country on linguistic lines would result
in still more partitions of the country. It was with great
reluctance that linguistic states began to be created
after Independence, beginning with Andhra Pradesh in
1953. A few more linguistic states were created in 1956.
Maharashtra and Gujarat were created in 1960 and
Punjab and Haryana in 1966. In almost all of these cases,
the states were only created after large-scale popular
movements that demanded their creation.

DOES A LANGUAGE BELONG TO A NATION?

Can a language actually 'belong' to a nation, a community, a people? Does English belong only to England, for instance? Or Japanese to Japan? What does 'belonging' actually mean?

Belonging only means that a certain language is spoken by a nation, a community or a people. It is their medium of expression. This is perhaps the best way to understand this.

In almost all cases, languages are older than nations. The borders of modern-day nations are not older than a few hundred years at most. Most languages are far older than that. So, to think of a language as 'belonging' to a nation is not accurate. It is better to think of a language as being spoken or used extensively in a certain nation or by a certain community or people.

So, when we list the languages of India, the idea is not to claim that they 'belong' to India. It is just to communicate that the languages are used extensively in India. As you will see later in the book, many 'Indian' languages are also used by people in other nations.

WHEN LANGUAGES 'DIE' . . .

When Thak Bahadur Majhi died in the Jorethan district of Sikkim in 2016, a language died with him.[6] He was the last speaker of the Majhi language. Though there are about a thousand members of the community still alive, none of them know more than a few words in their language. Most of them speak Nepali, the dominant language of Sikkim.

---

[6] 'Last speaker of Majhi language dead', 22 July 2016, https://timesofindia.indiatimes.com/City/Vadodara/Last-speaker-of-Majhi-language-dead/articleshow/53329911.cms

Why do languages 'die'?

Languages die for many cultural, political and social reasons. When speakers of a language spoken by a small number of people migrate to another place where nobody understands their language, they may decide that for survival it would be better to teach the language of the place they have migrated to, to their children.

Sometimes, when outsiders come to a region where a certain language is spoken and outnumber the locals, the local language is less and less understood, and as a result, people might stop speaking it. This does not happen overnight. But often, as in the case of Majhi, people realize that something has been lost only after losing it when it is too late to do anything.

In the past, often languages were 'forbidden' by kings and governments. As a result, the languages died out.

What happens when a language 'dies'?

When a language dies, many things happen. A language carries knowledge about local ecology, weather patterns, histories, mythology and culture. All of that is lost. That's what happened in 2010 when Boa Sr., the last speaker of the Bo language died in the Andamans.[7] She was the last link to a culture that went back about 65,000 years. She knew a number of songs and stories in Bo, none of which were understood by anyone else.

We lose a unique form of expression. Each language has its own vocabulary and distinct ways of description. For instance, people living in a windy region might have words for different types of

---

[7] Jonathan Watts, 'Ancient tribal language becomes extinct as last speaker dies', 4 February 2010, https://www.theguardian.com/world/2010/feb/04/ancient-language-extinct-speaker-dies

wind. Those in a cold region will have words to describe different stages of ice and snow. These are not fully translatable into any other language. This is lost.

Often, languages are treasure-troves of ecological information. They hold a lot of information about plants, animals and other information about natural resources in a region. In a time of climate change and ecological danger, this knowledge is especially precious.

When a language loses speakers, the last speakers of the language find fewer opportunities to speak in their mother tongue and communicate with the world. They are forced to rely on a language that is their second or third language which they might not be very fluent in.

How do we know a language is dying?

Languages die when the number of people speaking them falls steadily. There are about 6,000 to 7,000 languages in the world today. Most of these languages are spoken by less than 10,000 people and more importantly, many of them are not being taught to children. There is every possibility that many of these languages will die in the next few decades. In India, the Aimol language spoken in Manipur (6000 speakers), Bangani from Uttarakhand (6000 speakers) and Nihali from Madhya Pradesh and Maharashtra (2000 speakers) are some of the languages which are in danger of disappearing in the next few decades.[8]

Some linguists believe that fifty per cent of the world's languages will die in the next century. In the last hundred years, an estimated

---

[8] 'More than 40 languages may be heading for extinction: Officials', 19 February 2018, https://thewire.in/culture/more-than-40-languages-may-be-heading-for-extinction-officials

400 languages have died—one every three months. Many languages have fewer than ten speakers.

Even though the forecast is not very good for many languages, there is hope that technology might help in finding a solution by enabling others to learn the language or preserving the language for someone to learn it in the future.

DRAVIDIAN LANGUAGES

Dravidian languages are spoken by about twenty per cent of India's population. There are about thirty Dravidian languages, almost all of them in India. The four major languages of Tamil, Telugu, Kannada and Malayalam are the dominant tongues of southern India. Pockets of Dravidian language speakers are also found in central and eastern India. Interestingly, a Dravidian language (Brahui) is also spoken in Pakistan.

Some other Dravidian languages:

1. Tulu
2. Toda
3. Kolami
4. Malto
5. Gondi

TAMIL

The Dravidian pillar

On 21 October 1880, U.V. Swaminatha Iyer, a Tamil teacher and scholar employed in the Government Arts College at Kumbakonam (in today's Tamil Nadu) met Ramaswami Mudaliar, a judge recently posted to Kumbakonam. Mudaliar who was also a Tamil scholar, quizzed Iyer about his knowledge of Tamil literature. As Iyer rattled off the names of the Tamil works that he had spent years mastering, Mudaliar remained unimpressed since Iyer in his opinion hadn't read the *really important* ones—the *Jeevaka Chintamani,* the *Silappadikaram* and other ancient Tamil works. Iyer, on his part, was aghast that he hadn't even heard of them.

This chance meeting altered the way in which Tamil scholars and later, Tamilians, viewed the language and its history. Over the next few decades, Iyer proceeded on an epic quest to hunt for and publish many long-forgotten Tamil works. Many of these ancient works had been deliberately ignored and forced into oblivion by scholars in the seventeenth and eighteenth centuries because they were not religious in their content or were Buddhist or Jain works. But miraculously, many of the texts had survived—

in temples, in the dark corners of homes and other unlikely places—preserved by people who didn't really understand their importance. One bundle of palm-leaf manuscripts was found in a basket in a corner of the monastery where Iyer himself had studied!

The rediscovery of many of these works changed the perception of Tamil as it was then. It pushed the known origins of the language and its literature to a much earlier time and laid the foundation for a very different view of Indian languages.

ORIGINS AND EARLY LITERATURE

Tamil's place in the Indian language pantheon is an important one. Many people once believed (a few still do) that Sanskrit was the ancestor of *all* Indian languages. Scholars of Tamil were among the earliest to contest this and state that the Dravidian languages evolved independently of Sanskrit. They asserted the separate origins and history of the Dravidian languages and resisted being bracketed with Sanskrit.

Was Tamil, or at least an identifiably Dravidian tongue, the language of the Indus Valley civilization (the zenith of which was between 2600 BCE and 1700 BCE) as some scholars claim? Since the Indus Valley script has still not been deciphered, this is difficult to state with certainty. But we do know that even in early Vedic times (around 1500 BCE), some kind of Dravidian language, sometimes identified as Proto-Dravidian, was in existence. Scholars have identified many words of Dravidian origin in the Rig Veda (and at least one Dravidian word in the Hebrew Bible). By 1000 BCE, it can be stated with certainty that

Tamil existed in south India and perhaps in parts of the north too.

> Three Indic-derived words have been identified in the Hebrew Bible— *shenhabim* (ivory) derived from *shen* (a Semitic language word meaning tooth) and *ibha* (Sanskrit for elephant), *kofim* (meaning monkey from the Sanskrit *kapi*—this word came to Sanskrit from Munda) and *tukkiyim* (meaning parrots from the Tamil *tokai*, which means peacock's tail).

The earliest extant Tamil inscriptions date back to the second century BCE. They are written in the Southern Brahmi script, which may have been derived from the Ashokan script or the Northern Brahmi script of the third century BCE. Recently, evidence has emerged that seems to suggest that Southern Brahmi is older, possibly dating back to the fifth or fourth century BCE, but this is not yet fully confirmed.

The story of Tamil literature begins with what is termed as Sangam literature by historians today. Historians trace back these works to between 300 BCE and 300 or 400 CE. Of these, the *Tolkappiyam* is perhaps the earliest. The *Tolkappiyam* (which some historians argue was written around 200 BCE), composed by Tolkappiyar, is a grammatical work and therefore it must have been preceded by centuries of literary activity thus giving us an idea of how old Tamil possibly is. The *Silappadikaram* (The Tale of the Anklet) composed by Ilango Adigal is the latest, probably composed between 200 and 500 CE. Besides these two, there are the poetry anthologies *Patthupattu* (The Ten Idylls) and the *Ettuthokai* (The Eight Collections).

TIMELINE OF OTHER EARLY LITERARY TEXTS[9]

2500–1400 BCE: The *Epic of Gilgamesh* (Mesopotamia)

2000–1500 BCE: The Rigveda

1000–500 BCE: The Hebrew Bible (Israel)

800–700 BCE: The Iliad and the Odyssey (Greece)

6th century BCE: *The Art of War* (China)

500 BCE: Ramayana

400–200 BCE: Mahabharata

200 BCE: *Tolkappiyam*

Sangam literature, especially poetry, speaks through signs and symbols which have to be decoded. The poetry of this time is classified by theme into two kinds: *akam* (love poems) and *puram* (poems on war, kings, death and loss).

The Sangam Era is named after the assembly (sangam) of poets which took place in the ancient past. Legends say that there were three sangams. The first sangam 'sat' for 4,440 years and was presided over by the sage Agastya, the legendary creator of Tamil. It was convened in a city south of Madurai that myths say was later swallowed by the sea. The second sangam was

---

[9] *Source:* Brittanica.com and *World Literature I: Beginnings to 1650* by Laura Getty, Rhonda Kelley, Kyounghye Kwan and Douglass Thomson

in another legendary city called Kapatapuram. This sangam 'sat' for 3,700 years before Kapatapuram was destroyed by a flood. The *Tolkappiyam* is said to date back to this sangam. All the other works of the first two sangams have been lost. What we have today is from the third sangam in Madurai, in the first or second century CE. Tradition holds that this sangam 'sat' for 1,850 years.

Then there is the *Padinenkilkanakku* (The Eighteen Minor Poems), part of which is *Tirukkural* by Thiruvalluvar, a work on ethics and morality, probably composed around 450 CE, though some scholars attribute an earlier date. These are post-Sangam works.

Many of the works that Swaminatha Iyer rescued from oblivion were Sangam works and they helped establish how old Tamil really was.

THE STORY OF *SILAPPADIKARAM*

Silappadikaram begins in Puhar (Poompuhar), the ancient port town that is the capital of the Chola kingdom. Ships of all kinds sail in and out of its harbour to Sri Lanka, Burma and even distant Java and foreigners are forever crowding its markets looking for things to buy. Kovalan, the son of one of Puhar's most prominent and wealthy merchants, marries Kannagi. The young couple set up home and are very much in love before Kovalan deserts his wife for a dancer, Madhavi. Though saddened by Kovalan's action, Kannagi puts up with the indignity.

Some years later, suspecting Madhavi of infidelity, Kovalan returns to Kannagi, who large-heartedly welcomes him back.

By now, Kovalan has frittered away his fortune. The couple move to Madurai, the capital of the Pandyas, to rebuild their life. All that Kovalan and Kannagi have left are a pair of anklets. Kovalan offers one of the anklets to the royal goldsmith for sale. The goldsmith implicates Kovalan in the theft of the queen's anklet and Kovalan is swiftly executed. Kannagi confronts the king with her other anklet and proves that Kovalan was no thief as the queen's anklet contains pearls whereas hers contained gems.

Devastated, the king and queen die of remorse and guilt. When Kannagi walks out of the palace, her rage sets the entire city of Madurai on fire. On the advice of the guardian deity of Madurai, Kannagi undertakes a journey to Kodungallur in the Chera kingdom, from where she attains salvation.

THE CHOLA ERA

The next high point in the history of the Tamil region came when the Cholas reached the peak of their power under Rajaraja Chola I (ruled 985-1014 CE) and his son, Rajendra Chola I (reigned 1014-1044 CE).

The Cholas were an ancient dynasty of rulers. They are mentioned in the edicts of Ashoka (ruled 268-232 BCE) and along with the Pandyas and Cheras, two other important early Tamil dynasties, also find mention in Sangam literature.

During the time of Rajaraja, the Cholas established an empire that covered much of south India and northern Sri Lanka. However, their cultural and commercial influence extended far beyond the extent of their empire to encompass many parts of southeast Asia as well. The

Chola naval fleet, probably the most powerful of its time, extended the region of Chola influence to parts of Burma, Malaya, Cambodia, Laos and the island of Sumatra (in modern-day Indonesia) where the Srivijaya empire reigned. The Cholas also established trade relations with China (the Chinese referred to Rajaraja as Lots'a Lots'a). During this time, an influential and wealthy Tamil community established itself across the region and Tamil as a language began to be spoken wherever the Cholas went, not only by Tamil migrants but also by the natives of the other regions, indicating how important the language had become.

During this time, Tamil was the court language in the Chola court and literature flourished. The *Jeevaka Chintamani*, the work that Swaminatha Iyer hadn't heard of, was a Jain work written in the early tenth century by Tiruttakkatevar. The *Ramavataram*, which is the Tamil Ramayana written by Kamban, was composed around 1200 CE. Both are Chola-era works.

Ponniyin Selvan, a series of historical novels in five parts, written by Kalki Krishnamoorthy and published between 1950 and 1954 tells the story of the rise of Rajaraja Chola. This work, also available in English translation, has been made into a two-part movie released in 2022 and 2023.

By the time the Chola era ended around 1300 CE, the influence of Tamil had spread considerably. In the port town of Quanzhou in southern China, a bilingual Tamil-Chinese inscription talks about the establishment of a Shiva temple in the city in 1281 CE. This discovery is proof that Tamils were active in maritime trade a thousand years ago. Across many parts of southeast Asia, the traditional New Year is celebrated around the middle of April, which is also the new year according to the Tamil calendar. Very likely, this practice is a result of the Chola maritime influence.

> The modern-day Tamil script evolved from the Brahmi, Grantha, Vattezhutu and Pallava scripts. Brahmi is the oldest Indian script for which historical evidence is available. It was originally thought to have been invented in the times of Ashoka (third century BCE). However, recent evidence from excavations in Tamil Nadu suggests that it is even older (sixth or fifth century BCE). Tamil was originally written in Brahmi. Later, around the fourth century CE, the Vattezuthu script also began to be used, along with the Grantha and Pallava scripts. Vattezuthu, Pallava and Grantha are all related to Brahmi. The modern script reflects the influence of all these different scripts.

TAMIL IN THE MODERN ERA

In the nineteenth century, Tamil was studied deeply by the British. In 1816, Francis Whyte Ellis, the collector of Madras (now Chennai), wrote an academic article that stated that Tamil, Telugu, Kannada and Malayalam formed a distinct family of languages, separate from Sanskrit and Sanskrit-derived languages. In 1856, Robert Caldwell wrote *A Comparative Grammar of the Dravidian or South Indian Family of Languages*, where he proposed the name 'Dravidian' for this family of languages. This word had been used in the *Lilatilakam*, a fourteenth

HISTORY OF

நூற்றுண்டு CENTURY	a	ā	i	ī	u	ū	e	ē	ai	o	ō
	அ	ஆ	இ	ஈ	உ	ஊ	எ	ஏ	ஐ	ஒ	ஓ
BC 3rd C											
AD 2nd C											
AD 3rd C											
AD 4th C											
AD 5th C											
AD 6th C											
AD 7th C											
AD 8th C											
AD 9th C											
AD 10th C											
AD 11th C											
AD 12th C											
AD 13th C											
AD 14th C											
AD 15th C											
AD 16th C											
AD 17th C											
AD 18th C											
AD 19th C											

THE TAMIL SCRIPT

The history of Tamil script as displayed at Dakshina Chitra, Chennai.
(*Source*: https://en.wikipedia.org/wiki/Tamil_script#/media/File:History_of_Tamil_script.jpg)

or fifteenth-century work of Malayalam grammar (written in Sanskrit). It used the word 'Dramida' to refer to Tamil and Malayalam (it excluded Kannada and Telugu though).

Just like the *Lilatilakam* recognized that Tamil and Malayalam were very closely related, modern scholars also hold that Malayalam emerged from Tamil between 500 CE and 1000 CE. In Sangam literature, the region that is now Kerala is identified as being ruled by the Cheras and considered a part of *Tamilakam* (the Tamil region). Post 1000 CE, Malayalam developed independently of Tamil.

Kannada, along with Tamil, ranks as among the oldest of the Dravidian tongues. Ashoka's Brahmagiri edict which dates back to 250 BCE, the language of which is Prakrit and which is written in the Brahmi script, contains the word 'Isila', which has been identified as being of Kannada origin and proof that the language existed during that time and even earlier.

Tamil, Malayalam, and Kannada are closely related and belong to the South Dravidian sub-group. Telugu, Gondi, Chenchu and a few other languages, while related to Tamil and the other South Dravidian languages, are a little different and belong to the south-Central sub-group. There is also a Central Dravidian sub-group consisting of Kolami and Parji and a North Dravidian sub-group consisting of Brahui, Malto and other languages.

The British interest in Tamil ensured that the language was taught in the various schools and colleges they established. Swaminatha Iyer was a teacher in one such college. Owing to his work and the work of others like C.V. Damodaram Pillai and A. Narayanaswami Iyer, Tamil underwent a reassessment in the early twentieth century. Its sense of its own history underwent a shift, and it claimed parity with Sanskrit as an ancient and highly developed language that has evolved independently from Sanskrit and Sanskrit-derived languages.

The creation of Madras State (later renamed Tamil Nadu), with a majority Tamil population, in 1956 further strengthened the development of the language. Tamil literature and popular culture in the form of films and music are vibrant and thriving. Rajinikanth and Kamal Hassan, two well-known actors are among Tamil cinema's most loved. The works of the director, Pa. Ranjith (*Kabali* and *Kaala*, both starring Rajinikanth, and *Sarpatta Parambarai* are a few) have given Tamil cinema a new dimension in recent years. A.R. Rahman, the well-known music composer began his career in Tamil films with the movie *Roja*, released in 1992. In recent years, the writer, Perumal Murugan has become famous internationally for works like *Poonachi, One Part Woman, Fire Bird* and many others. *Hours Past Midnight* by Salma, who is also a poet, is another well-known Tamil novel that deals with women's issues.

Tamil has also attempted to modernize itself by developing a scientific and modern vocabulary that would enable it to become the language of higher education. It is extensively used in social media and has proved to be fairly resilient in its struggle to hold its own against both Hindi and English and now occupies a special place in the Indian language scenario.

TIMELINE

First millennium BCE: Great likelihood of the existence of a Dravidian language in south India.

300–350 CE: Sangam Era.

1000: Chola Era. Tamil is the court language.

1200: Tamil Ramayana written by Kamban.

1281: Bilingual Tamil-Chinese inscription records the establishment of a Shiva Temple in Quanzhou, China.

1816: Francis Whyte Ellis writes about Tamil, Kannada, Telugu and Malayalam being a distinct family of languages.

1856: Robert Caldwell proposes the name 'Dravidian'.

1956: Creation of Madras State (later Tamil Nadu) with a majority Tamil population.

As per the latest estimates, there are about eighty million speakers of Tamil worldwide.[10]

---

[10] *Source:* https://www.ethnologue.com/language/tam/

TELUGU
A language of melody

Kakunuri Appakavi was a renowned Telugu poet and grammarian of the seventeenth century. One night in 1656 CE, Lord Vishnu appeared to him in his dream and said:

Make Nannayya's book into Telugu, with my help,
to the poets' astonishment and praise.
Don't ask me how you turn into Telugu
a book you've never heard or seen. I'll tell you
all about that book and how it will come to you.[11]

Vishnu told Appakavi the following morning that a brahmin from Matanga Hill in Hampi would visit him and give him a copy of Nannayya's work.

Nannayya was a Telugu poet and grammarian from the eleventh century CE and the author of the *Andhra Mahabharatam*, a Telugu retelling of the Mahabharata.

---

[11] Velcheru Narayana Rao, and David Shulman, translators, editors and with an introduction by. 'On Poetry and Grammar', *Classical Telugu Poetry: An Anthology.* (Berkeley, Calif: University of California Press)

This is the oldest literary work in the language that is recorded. In addition to *Mahabharatam*, legend had it that he had also written a Sanskrit work on Telugu grammar, entitled *Andhra Shabda Chintamani*. The only copy of the grammar had supposedly been thrown into the Godavari by Nannayya's rival, Bhimakavi. But Bhimakavi did not know that Nannayya's disciple, Sarangadhara, had memorized it.

Sarangadhara was the son of Rajarajanarendra, Nannayya's patron who was a local ruler. Rajarajnarendra had married a young woman in his old age. The young queen fell in love with her stepson, Sarangadhara. When Sarangadhara refused to reciprocate, the queen levelled false charges against Sarangadhara. The king then cut off his arms and legs and exiled him to the jungle. Miraculously, Sarangadhara survived with the help of a *siddha* yogi.[12] Sarangadhara also became a siddha yogi and hence attained immortality.

Centuries later, Sarangadhara made a written copy of Nannayya's work and gave it to Balasarasvati, Appakavi's contemporary, near Matanga Hill, at Hampi. This was then delivered to Appakavi whose elaboration of Nannayya's work in Telugu became the *Appakaviyamu.*

Nannayya is renowned as Telugu's first poet (*Aadi Kavi*) and is held in high regard for reviving the Telugu language. Since there was no Telugu grammar to dictate proper use of the language (Nannayya's grammar was lost), the poets who followed Nannayya had decided to not use any word

---

[12] Siddha yogis are considered 'accomplished beings' who have achieved spiritual perfection (enlightenment). They are believed to have attained immortality.

which was not in the *Andhra Mahabharatam*. This was a particularly difficult rule to follow since only two-and-a-half chapters of Nannayya's work had been written before Nannayya passed away. Therefore, the number of words was limited.

Hence by Appakavi's time, the need was felt for a grammar that would enable the further development of Telugu poetry and writing. This resulted in the *Appakaviyamu,* which is an original work though it claims to be a commentary on an earlier work.

The story of how Appakavi came to write his work by getting hold of Nannayya's work is a figment of Appakavi's own imagination. But Nannayya and Appakavi are real people. Sarangadhara was real too, though not immortal. This story about how he had attained immortality and made a written copy of Nannayya's work was perhaps created because Telugu writers wanted to do more with the language, but the restriction on using words only from Nannayya's work was an obstacle. Through the creation of a new work, the language could progress. But to create a work which would overcome that obstacle, this story was used to change the way things were.

BEGINNINGS AND GROWTH

Telugu's origins go back centuries before Nannayya. Historians have discovered Prakrit inscriptions with Telugu words dating between 400 BCE and 100 BCE and have estimated that Telugu's origins probably go back even earlier to 1500 BCE to 1000 BCE. This was the period when the ancestor of all Dravidian languages called Proto-Dravidian was prevalent. Telugu emerged from Proto-Dravidian, and at about the same time, Tamil and probably Kannada too began to emerge as independent languages.

The earliest Telugu inscription has been dated to 575 CE and was found in Kadapa district, Andhra Pradesh. It was issued by the Renati Cholas (sometimes spelt Chodas), who were the first rulers of the region to issue inscriptions in Telugu, instead of Sanskrit. There are many more inscriptions dating to later centuries from different parts of what are today the states of Telangana and Andhra Pradesh. Eventually, in the eleventh century, Nannayya wrote the first Telugu literary work, though he could not complete it.

> According to Telugu myth and folklore, the sage Kanva was said to have written the first grammar of Telugu. There are about twenty sayings about grammar that are ascribed to him. Scholars believe that Kanva very likely wrote an ancient Telugu grammar that was lost.

Tikkanna (1205–88) completed most of the Mahabharatha begun by Nannayya (he did not finish it though) and wrote other works as well. Interestingly, since Nannayya had died when writing the third chapter of the Mahabharatha, that chapter came to be considered inauspicious. Tikkanna's Mahabharatha, therefore, begins from the fourth chapter. Unlike Nannayya, whose Telugu was highly influenced by Sanskrit, Tikkanna wrote in more chaste Telugu and did not use too many Sanskrit words or expressions. It was Erranna (1325–53) who finally completed the Telugu Mahabharatha. Together, Nannayya, Tikkanna and Erranna are known as the *kavitrayam* (Trinity of Poets).

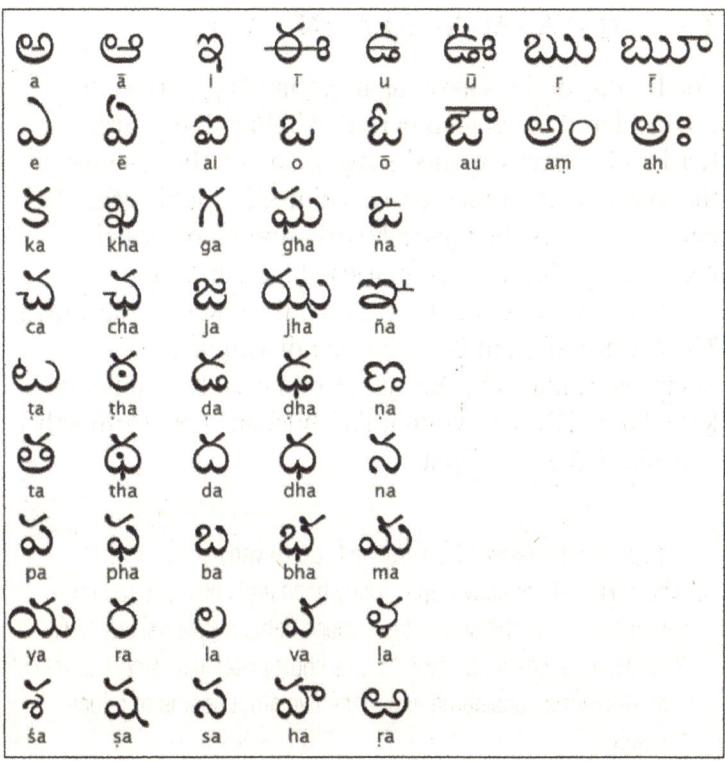

అ a	ఆ ā	ఇ i	ఈ ī	ఉ u	ఊ ū	బు r̥	బూ r̥̄
ఎ e	ఏ ē	ఐ ai	ఒ o	ఓ ō	ఔ au	అం aṃ	అః aḥ
క ka	ఖ kha	గ ga	ఘ gha	ఙ ṅa			
చ ca	ఛ cha	జ ja	ఝ jha	ఞ ña			
ట ṭa	ఠ ṭha	డ ḍa	ఢ ḍha	ణ ṇa			
త ta	థ tha	ద da	ధ dha	న na			
ప pa	ఫ pha	బ ba	భ bha	మ ma			
య ya	ర ra	ల la	వ va	ళ ḷa			
శ śa	ష ṣa	స sa	హ ha	ఱ ṟa			

The Telugu script

The modern-day Telugu script is historically connected to Brahmi. The Bhattiprolu script, which has been found on some old inscriptions, dating to between the third and first centuries BCE, evolved from Brahmi. This script influenced the Kadamba script from which the Telugu and Kannada scripts evolved. The Telugu and Kannada scripts are very similar and are more or less mutually intelligible.

THE VIJAYANAGAR ERA AND AFTER

The heyday of the Vijayanagar empire (1336–1565 CE) is considered the golden period of Telugu literature. Krishnadevaraya (reigned 1509–1529 CE), the greatest of the Vijayanagar emperors, was himself a highly regarded poet who wrote the poetical work, *Amuktamalayada*. Eight Telugu literary luminaries—together called the *Ashtadiggajas*—adorned the court of Krishnadevaraya. These were Allasani Peddana, Nandi Timmanna, Madayagari Mallana, Dhurjati, Ayyalaraju Ramabhadra Kavi, Pingali Surana, Ramaraja Bhushana (Bhattumurthi) and Tenali Ramakrishna.

In popular lore, Tenali Ramakrishna is portrayed as someone who tickled Krishnadevaraya's funny bone and conveyed to him through his jests the short-sightedness of his decisions. But Tenali Ramakrishna was much more than a court jester. His *Panduranga Mahatmyam* is considered one of the five great poems of Telugu literature.

Telugu literature later flourished under the Qutb Shahi dynasty (1518–1687 CE), even though their court language was Persian. Similarly, when the Telugu-speaking Nayakas ruled Madurai (1529–1736) and Thanjavur (1532–1673), both located in a Tamil-speaking region, Telugu literature flourished under their patronage. This was not an unusual situation for Telugu. The capital of the Vijayanagar empire, Hampi, in modern-day Karnataka, was in a Kannada-speaking region. Krishnadevaraya even called himself a 'Kannadaraya' (Kannada king). Despite that, Telugu received patronage and its writers flourished. In contrast, some of the dynasties situated in Telugu-speaking regions often preferred patronizing Sanskrit literature instead of Telugu.

It is said that the Italian explorer, Niccolo Da Conti, who visited Vijayanagar, termed Telugu the 'Italian of the East' because of its melodic sounds which reminded him of his own language, which was also known for its musical cadences.

TELUGU IN THE MODERN ERA

Charles Philip (C.P.) Brown (1798–1884), a civil servant in the East India Company, is held in high regard in the history of Telugu in the British era. In 1820, when Thomas Munro, the Governor of Madras, instructed all civil service officers to learn a local language, Brown chose to learn Telugu. Later, he served in the revenue and judicial departments in Kadapa and Masulipatnam. Brown developed an abiding interest in the language and studied it deeply.

Brown contributed to Telugu in three different ways. He developed a large collection of old Telugu manuscripts. He then published many of them, along with a commentary to enable ordinary people to understand them. He also wrote several works on Telugu, including a dictionary and a grammar. This focus on Telugu was critical at a time when Telugu literature appeared to be dying out due to the lack of royal patronage. Brown's vigorous efforts to revive the language played an important part in the renaissance of Telugu literature in the nineteenth and twentieth centuries when people like K.V. Pantulu, Gurajada Appa Rao and many others introduced the novel, short stories and European-style drama to Telugu literature.

When Indian independence came in 1947, Telugu speakers were scattered in many different provinces and princely states. Hyderabad under the Nizam was one such princely state. Besides Hyderabad, there were other princely kingdoms like Bobbili and Vizianagaram. Telugu speakers were also found in large numbers in parts of the Madras Presidency.

The expectation among Telugu speakers in the Madras Presidency was the creation of a separate Telugu-majority state from the Telugu-speaking districts of the province. However, the central government, for various reasons, delayed the creation of a separate Andhra state even after announcing that it intended to do so.

Between October and December 1952, Potti Sriramulu, a freedom fighter and social activist fasted non-stop for fifty-six days demanding the creation of a separate Andhra. He eventually died on 15 December 1952, prompting the then prime minister, Jawaharlal Nehru to announce the creation of a separate Andhra state which came into being in October 1953. This was the first of the linguistic states of independent India.

POTTI SRIRAMULU (1901–52)

Sriramulu was an employee of the Railways. After leaving his job, he became an ardent follower of Mahatma Gandhi and took part in the independence movement and was imprisoned for participating in the 1930 Salt Satyagraha. He also participated in the Quit India movement and was imprisoned thrice.

Between 1943 and 1944, he worked for the widespread adoption of *charkha* spinning. He undertook three fasts between 1946 and 1948, in support of Dalit rights to enter temples. He is today revered as an *Amarajeevi* (immortal being) in Telugu-speaking regions.

In November 1956, the Telugu-speaking districts of Hyderabad were merged with Andhra to form a united Andhra Pradesh. In 2014, Andhra Pradesh was split into two states: Telangana and Andhra Pradesh. Both states continue to have a Telugu-speaking majority. Telugu speakers are also a majority in Yanam, which is part of the union territory of Pondicherry.

In recent years, Telugu cinema, popularly called Tollywood, has gained enormous popularity nationally. *Baahubali* released in 2015 became extremely popular both in India and in other parts of the world. It has spawned sequels and web series spinoffs. Another Telugu movie that made a huge splash worldwide was *RRR*, released in 2022, whose song 'Naatu Naatu' won an Academy (Oscar) award.

Contemporary Telugu literature has a large readership. The poetry of Sri Sri and Devulapalli Krishna Sastri, though written many decades ago, continues to be popular. The feminist works of Popuri Lalitha Kumari, better known by her pseudonym, Volga, have given a new dimension to Telugu literature. Among Telugu literature's more unusual figures is Gaddar, a popular performer-singer who was extremely popular for his poems which he usually sang in political functions and rallies.

Telugu's closest relative is Gondi. The Gonds are a tribe found mostly in Andhra Pradesh, Telangana, Madhya Pradesh, Chhattisgarh and Maharashtra. While there are an estimated eleven to fifteen million Gonds, only about three million speak the language. Gondi, which has a rich oral tradition, is mostly written in the Telugu and Devanagari scripts. The Masaram Gondi script, which was created by Munshi Mangal Singh Masaram of Madhya Pradesh in 1918, is also sometimes used. It was adopted as the official script for the Gondi language in Maharashtra in 2011. Some years ago, researchers discovered eighteenth-century Gondi manuscripts written in another script known as Gunjala Gondi.

TIMELINE

400–100 BCE: Prakrit inscriptions with Telugu words were inscribed.

575 CE: The earliest Telugu inscription.

11th century: Nannayya wrote parts of the *Andhra Mahabharatam*, a Telugu retelling of the Mahabharata.

1200s: Tikkanna (1205–88) completed most of the Mahabharatha begun by Nannayya.

1300s: Erranna (1325–53) completed the Telugu Mahabharatha.

1336–1565: The Vijayanagar period, the golden period of Telugu literature.

19th century: The era of C.P. Brown (1798–1884).

15 December 1952: Potti Sriramulu dies after fasting for fifty-six days for the creation of a separate Andhra.

October 1953: Andhra state is created.

November 1956: Telugu-speaking districts of Hyderabad merged with Andhra to form Andhra Pradesh.

2014: Andhra Pradesh split into two states: Telangana and Andhra Pradesh, both with majority Telugu speakers.

As per the latest estimates, there are about ninety million speakers of Telugu worldwide.[13]

---

[13] *Source:* https://www.ethnologue.com/language/tel/

BRAHUI

A slice of south India in Pakistan

Two thousand kilometres from the Dravidian language speaking states of southern India lies Balochistan, Pakistan's largest province in terms of area and smallest in terms of population. Here, Balochi and Pashto, both languages of the Indo-European family, are the most widely spoken languages. And then there is also Brahui, a language connected to the Dravidian tongues of distant southern India!

Brahui is spoken by an estimated 2.5 million people around the world, but the majority of speakers are in Pakistani Balochistan. Small groups are also found in Iranian Balochistan, Afghanistan and Turkmenistan. This language doesn't have any connections with those spoken around it, which are largely Indo-European.

Why is there a Dravidian language spoken in an area where the other prominent languages are Indo-European? This mystery has spawned a variety of theories.

Some experts believe that the Brahuis are the descendants of the people of the Indus Valley civilization (centred in Punjab and Sindh), which some argue was

Dravidian. When the civilization disappeared for reasons that are still entirely unclear, a group made its way westward to Balochistan, where they preserved their ancient language.

Another theory is that Dravidian speakers were also migrants to the subcontinent and the Brahui speakers are those who stayed on in Balochistan and did not move to southern India. A third theory suggests that the Brahuis moved to their current area from southern India around the twelfth century. Conclusive proof does not exist for any of these theories.

The Brahuis as a people first find mention in recorded history when the Khanate of Kalat was founded by Mir Ahmad Khan Qambrani around 1666 and became a separate principality under the Mughal empire. The principality was absorbed into Balochistan in 1955. The last ruler was Mir Ahmad Yar Khan Ahmadzai Baloch. The Khans of Kalat were Brahui speakers in private, though their court language was Baloch as it was spoken by the majority of their subjects.

At present, twenty-seven tribes constitute the Brahui universe. But not all those who identify as Brahuis are necessarily Brahui speakers. Brahui is also a term for a group of tribes—some speak Brahui, some are bilingual in Brahui and Baloch, and some are exclusively Baloch-speaking. A Brahui tribal and a Brahui speaker do not refer to the same group of people. This makes it hard to form accurate estimates of the number of Brahui speakers.

Brahui's difference from the languages spoken around it was first noted by Henry Pottinger, a British soldier who later became the first governor of Hong Kong, in 1816. In 1880, Ernest Trumpp, a German missionary, published the first scientific study of the language and identified it conclusively as Dravidian. In 1909, Denys Bray published a grammar and dictionary that is still regarded as a definitive one.

Today, Brahui is classified under the North Dravidian sub-group along with Kurukh or Oraon (spoken in Jharkhand and West Bengal) and Malto (spoken in Bihar and West Bengal).

When one looks at the many similarities between certain Brahui words and words used in other Dravidian languages, the connection is clear. A few Brahui words that are clearly Dravidian in origin are listed below:

Today: *Aino* (Brahui), *Inru* (Tamil) *Innu* (Malayalam)

You: *Ne* (Brahui), *Nee* (Tamil, Malayalam)

Come: *Baa* (Brahui), *Vaa* (Tamil, Malayalam)

Snore: *Khurkao* (Brahui), *Khurattai* (Tamil)

Eye: *Xan* (Brahui), *Kan* (Tamil)

Stone: *Xal* (Brahui), *Kal* (Tamil)

Milk: *Pal* (Brahui), *Pal* (Tamil)

News: *Haval* (Brahui), *Thahaval* (Tamil)

For its numbering system, Brahui draws from a Dravidian source for two (*irat*, similar to the Kannada *eradu*) and three (*musit*, akin to the Tamil *moonru* and the Kannada *mooru*) but from four onwards, the words are all Indo-Aryan borrowings (*char*, *paanch* and so on). The Brahui word for one (*asit*) seems to have no connection with any other language.

Owing to its long isolation from other Dravidian languages, most Brahui words are drawn from the Indo-European languages around it, like Balochi, Persian, Sindhi and Urdu. Some experts estimate that only about fifteen per cent of its vocabulary is now Dravidian. Hence, a Tamil speaker and a Brahui speaker are unlikely to understand each other. But experts have also noted that Balochi words, too, have been taken from Brahui.

Since Brahui is essentially a spoken language, and its speakers are mostly illiterate, its literary tradition is not a very developed one. The first written work in Brahui was *Tuhfat-al-ajaib* (The Gift of Wonders) written around 1759–60 by Malikdad Gharsin Qalati. The original manuscript has been lost and what exists today has been taken from a 1916 print edition. In the late nineteenth century, a standard script was also created for Brahui based on the Perso-Arabic system (used for Urdu and other languages) that was in use for the other languages of the region. Publishing efforts in Brahui have been limited on account of poor literacy levels. The Brahui Academy, founded in 1966, and located in Quetta, the capital of Balochistan, publishes some books in the language. The sole magazine, *Ilum* (Brother) is also still published.

Today, Brahui is listed by UNESCO as an 'endangered' language. Its speakers seem to be dwindling and this poses a real threat to the language's continued existence. By and large, Pakistan's language policy favours Urdu due to political and historical reasons and this has marginalized the other native languages of the country (which number about seventy-five).

If Brahui were to vanish, it would be a cultural tragedy as its existence reminds us that the world is far more interconnected than we think.

TIMELINE

17th century: The Brahuis first appear in history when the Khanate of Kalat becomes a separate principality under Mughal rule in 1666.

1759–60: The first written work in Brahui, *Tuhfat-al-ajaib* by Malikdad Gharsin Qalati.

1816: Brahui's difference from the languages spoken around it is first noticed by Henry Pottinger, a British soldier.

1880: Ernest Trumpp, a German missionary, publishes the first scientific study of the language and identifies it as Dravidian.

1909: Denys Bray publishes a grammar and dictionary of the language.

1955: Kalat is absorbed into Balochistan.

1966: The Brahui Academy is founded in Quetta, the capital of Balochistan.

As per the latest estimates, Brahui is spoken by an estimated two and a half million people.[14]

---

[14] *Source:* https://www.ethnologue.com/language/brh/

AUTRO-ASIATIC LANGUAGES

There are about 170 Austro-Asiatic languages found all over southeast Asia and eastern India. Worldwide, Khmer (Cambodia), Mon (Myanmar) and Vietnamese are three of the most widely spoken languages in this family. In India, Khasi, Nicobarese and the Munda or Kolarian languages, the most important of which is Santali, are some of the widely spoken languages from this family. Some scholars believe that these languages might justifiably be called India's 'original' language group since they probably predate both the Dravidian and Indo-Aryan language groups. Till the nineteenth century, the Austro-Asiatic languages of India were only spoken tongues lacking a written script.

Some other Austro-Asiatic languages found in India are:

1. Korku
2. Kharia
3. Mundari
4. Ho
5. Sora

SANTALI

The most widely spoken tribal language

In 2003, Santali (sometimes spelt Santhali) was included in the list of scheduled languages in the Constitution of India, an important recognition of both the Santal community and its tongue. The long wait for this status to come to Santali tells us something about the complicated language politics of India.

The Santali-speaking population in India is large—the 2001 Census recorded 6.4 million speakers, which increased to 7.3 million speakers in the 2011 Census. But the majority of its speakers are spread across four states—Jharkhand (forty-four per cent of Santali speakers), West Bengal (thirty-three per cent), Odisha (twelve per cent) and Bihar (six per cent). In none of these states are Santali speakers a majority. This was largely why Santali was denied its due for a long time. Besides India, Santali speakers are also found in Nepal and Bangladesh.

THE PEOPLE AND THEIR HISTORY

Santali is the predominant language of the Santals, India's largest tribal community.

Scholars believe that the Santals came to the Indian subcontinent in prehistoric times, probably much before the people whom we today call the Aryans and the Dravidians. The oral traditions of the Santals also suggest a history of migration. Their tales refer to places with names like 'Hihiri Pihiri', 'Khoj Kaman', 'Harata' and 'Sasangbeda' as areas where they had lived in the past. At some point in time, they also lived in 'Champa', where the legends say they lived under their own ruler. It is unclear, though, where these locations are.

> The Santal myth of creation states that in the beginning there was only water and soil. Thakur Jiu (Supreme God) first created animals. Thakur Jiu then created a human couple from the soil. Sin Sadom (the sun in the form of a horse) came down from the skies and trampled them to pieces. But Thakur Jiu recreated them.
>
> The first human couple grew up in Hihiri Pipiri, the original birthplace of the Santals. A Santal song says that Hihiri Pipiri was paradise, where the first human beings were taken care of by the birds according to the advice of Thakur Jiu. When the birds faced difficulties in feeding the human couple, Thakur Jiu created the whole universe for the wellbeing of humankind. Hence, the earth has been created as the source of life for all human beings.

Since Santali is an Austro-Asiatic language, it is likely that the ancestors of the Santals came from southeast Asia, where other Austro-Asiatic languages like Khmer, Mon and Vietnamese are found today. Eventually, they came to occupy parts of the Chota Nagpur plateau, which is spread across much of Jharkhand and parts of Chhattisgarh, West Bengal, Bihar and Odisha. They hunted game in the thick forests besides also practising some form of shifting cultivation.

The first recorded mention of the Santals is in an article published in 1795, where Sir John Shore, the governor-general of Bengal (1793–98), refers to them as 'Soontar' and as living in Ramgarh in today's Jharkhand. Other British accounts record their presence in many other parts of Jharkhand and Bengal. From 1790s up until 1810, the British relocated a number of Santals to the Rajmahal Hills region in another part of Jharkhand.

The reason behind this relocation was the demand for agricultural labour in the Rajmahal Hills. The Santals soon began to work as agricultural labourers and some also got land on lease. The region in which the Santals were relocated came to be known as 'Damin-i-koh'. This region soon attracted Santals from neighbouring districts. They thought that they would have a homeland of their own and preserve their culture and identity. But over the next few decades, this changed as more and more outsiders made their way into Santal territory. Merchants and traders often fleeced the Santals by paying them less than the fair price for their crops and overcharging them for oil, cloth and other commodities. Many Santals fell into debt as a result, creating a vicious cycle of exploitation.

Between June 1855 and January 1856, the Hul rebellion took place when the Santals in large numbers, led by the brothers Sidhu and Kanhu Murmu, rebelled. The rebellion began as a reaction against the moneylenders and merchants and eventually became a full-fledged war against the British. Though the Santals were hardy warriors, the superior firepower of the British forces overwhelmed them. Close to 20,000 Santals perished. Sidhu and Kanhu were captured and executed. Nevertheless, the British did introduce some reforms to give the tribals a modicum of protection against exploitation.

THE LITERATURE AND SCRIPT

For centuries, Santali was only a spoken language. Songs, rhymes, proverbs and stories narrated orally constituted its literature, giving its listeners a glimpse of Santali life. The first attempts to write the language were made in the nineteenth century. Since the Santals lived in different linguistic areas, a variety of scripts were used including Bangla, Devanagari, Odia and Roman.

Jeremiah Phillips, an American missionary, devised a writing system for Santali using the Bangla script. In 1852, he published *An Introduction to the Santal Language* and translated parts of the Bible, including the Gospel of Matthew, into Santali. He also produced a grammar and dictionary and opened a number of schools in the Chota Nagpur region.

Hor-ko-ren mare Harprarn-ko-reak Katha (The Traditions of the Ancestors of the Hor or Santal people) is a compilation of Santali stories and legends as narrated by a guru named Kolean. This narration was collected and published by a Norwegian missionary Lars Olsen Skrefrsud in 1887 in the Roman script. In 1873, Skresfrud had published a grammar of Santali. Another early compilation of Santali folk tales and their lives in the jungle was also made in the Roman script by another Norwegian missionary, Paul Olaf Budding. Budding also modified the Roman script so that it could accommodate the various Santali sounds. In 1914, he completed the translation of the Bible into Santali.

Kherwal-Vamsa Dharam-Puthi (The Sacred Book of the Kherwal Race)[15] was published in 1902 in the Bangla script. This was the work of Ramdas Majhi Tudu, who compiled the oral literature about the traditions of his people and their religious and social culture, besides including original work of his own.

In 1925, Pandit Raghunath Murmu (Guru Gomke) devised the Ol Chiki (Alchiki) script for the language. This, he felt, was necessary to be able to pronounce the language correctly which the Roman and Indian language scripts were not able to achieve. The script uses signs and symbols familiar to the Santals. The letters are derived from the environment that surrounds the Santal people—hills, rivers, trees, birds, bees, plough, and sickle. This ingenuity in shaping the symbols of the letters and arranging the letters in the script has been helpful in popularizing the script.

Guru Gomke also wrote a number of books in Ol Chiki in order to popularize the script, including grammar, novels, short stories, drama and poetry. *Darege Dhan, Sidhu-Kanhu, Bidu Chandan* and *Kherwal Bir* are among the most acclaimed of his works.

Modern Santali literature is well-developed and a number of books of all kinds are published every year.

---

[15] Kherwal is an old name for the Santals and other related tribal groups.

The Ol Chiki script[16]

Shibu Tudu is a contemporary Santali writer whose *Turui Maha* (Six Days, 2007), a non-fiction work on the importance of Sohrai, the harvest festival of the Santals, and *Tirla* (Teenage Girl, 2016), a poetry collection have become popular. Hansda Sowvendra Shekhar, a Santal writer who writes in English, has translated Shibu Tudu's work into English. Hansda's own collection of short stories (in English) entitled *The Adivasi Will Not Dance* is also a powerful portrayal of modern Santali life.

Santali is today a widely used language and is an additional official language in Jharkhand and West Bengal. It continues to struggle though to hold its own against Hindi and English. This is a struggle that is unlikely to ebb anytime soon.

---

[16] *Source:* https://kherwalbakhol.wordpress.com/ol-chiki/

TIMELINE

1795: First mention of Santals in a historical document.

1852: *An Introduction to the Santal Language* published by Jeremiah Phillips, who also devised a writing system using the Bangla script.

June 1855–January 1856: The Hul rebellion.

1873: Lars Olsen Skrefrsud publishes a Santali grammar.

1887: *Hor-ko-ren mare Harprarn-ko-reak Katha* collected and published by Skrefrsud in the Roman script.

1902: *Kherwal-Vamsa Dharam-Puthi* by Ramdas Majhi Tudu published in the Bangla script.

1914: Paul Olaf Budding completes the translation of *the Bible* into Santali.

1925: Pandit Raghunath Murmu (Guru Gomke) devises the Ol Chiki (Alchiki) script for the language.

2003: Santali included in the list of scheduled languages in the Constitution of India.

2018: Santali Wikipedia launched.

2022: Droupadi Murmu, a native Santali speaker, becomes President of India.

The Santali-speaking population in India is 7.3 million speakers, as per the 2011 Census.

KHASI
Thriving in the hills

On 21 January 1972, two districts from the state of
Assam—Khasi and Jaintia Hills and Garo Hills—were
separated to create a new state, Meghalaya.[17] The name
chosen, meaning 'abode of the clouds', had been first
used in 1936 by S.P. Chatterjee, an eminent professor of
geography who had worked in the region as a research
student. The largest community in this new state was the
Khasis, a matrilineal tribe that constituted the majority
in the Khasi Hills region. Besides Meghalaya, Khasis
are also found in Assam, Manipur, West Bengal and
Bangladesh.

The Khasis are believed to have been living in the
region for thousands of years, since the time a group of
their ancestors separated from the other Austro-Asiatic
language-speaking communities in southeast Asia and
moved to this area. Estimates of when this happened
begin from 12,000 years ago. To reach this region, they
had to come via Myanmar. The linguists deduce this

---

[17] There are twelve districts in Meghalaya now.

since the Palaung languages of Myanmar[18] are closely related to Khasi. This indicates that these languages probably go back to a common language, which was likely spoken by one community before one group travelled further and different languages emerged from the common language.

The Khasis are divided into seven groups or clans, each of which is identified with a specific geographic region. Each clan has a different name (such as Boi, War, Maram and others) and each is somewhat different from the others. But there are many similarities as well and together, they call themselves Khasi.

Khasis call their homeland *Ki Hynñiewtrep*, or the Land of Seven Huts. The Khasi mythology of creation talks of sixteen clans or families at the beginning of time, out of which seven came to earth and nine remained in heaven. For long, there was a bridge between heaven and earth until the seven families on earth committed the grave error of cutting a divine tree, because of which the links between heaven and earth snapped.

The Khasis are surrounded by communities speaking languages belonging to other language families—Indo-Aryan languages like Assamese and Bangla and Sino-Tibetan languages like Garo, Manipuri and Bodo. But the Khasi language continued to thrive. The geography of the region, with its hills and forests, kept the community relatively isolated from the world beyond the Khasi Hills

---

[18] There are three languages spoken by the Palaungic people found in Myanmar and China—Pale, Rumai and Shwe. All these languages are now considered endangered since the number of speakers is falling every year.

till the nineteenth century. The language, culture and traditions developed more or less independently for hundreds of years.

When the British first came to the Khasi region in 1823, after they conquered Assam, there were twenty-five kingdoms. The Khasis also had their own indigenous religion (*Niam Tynrai*, or traditional faith) that revolved around land, clan and family. While many Khasis are now Christians, as a result of the influx of missionaries from the nineteenth century onwards, the indigenous Khasi religion also survives. There are also Khasi Hindus, Muslims, Buddhists and atheists.

The Khasis follow a matrilineal system. The youngest daughter inherits all the property and responsibilities of the family. In case a family has no daughters, the family adopts a girl from another family. This system has been challenged in modern times, but the traditional system continues to be of importance.

THE LANGUAGE AND SCRIPT

Till the middle of the nineteenth century, Khasi was an oral language. Due to some limited contact with the outside world, some of the Khasi kingdoms kept written records and communicated with each other in the Khasi language written in the Bangla script. The English missionary, William Carey, also used the Bangla script to write the language in the 1820s and 1830s.

In 1841, the Welsh missionary, Reverend Thomas Jones came to the Khasi Hills. He studied the language and decided to use the Roman script for it. He also translated a part of the Bible (the Gospel of Matthew) into Khasi.

A B K D E G
Ng H I Ï J L
M N Ñ O P R
S T U W Y

The Khasi alphabet in the Roman script.[19]

Thomas Jones began the practice of using the Roman alphabet for Khasi. After some years, a special Roman alphabet was developed for Khasi. In the Khasi alphabet, the letters c, f, q, v, x and z were removed. Two special letters were added—'ï' and 'ñ' ('ï' is pronounced like 'Yi' in 'yeast' and 'ñ' is pronounced 'enya'). Another special letter has been created by combining 'n' and 'g' and 'ng' is treated as an independent letter of the alphabet. Interestingly, 'ng' is also used in the Welsh alphabet.

THE LITERATURE

For centuries, Khasi literature was oral. Folk tales were narrated and sometimes sung after a hard day's work in the rice fields or forests, often around the fire when

---

[19] Though only capital letters are shown here, the language also uses lowercase letters. (*Source:* https://theshillongtimes.com/2017/08/01/use-khasi-in-govt-offices/khasi-alphabets/)

the food was cooking. Many stories were meant to teach Khasi customs and social laws (*ki jingsneng tymmen*) to children. Later, when the Khasi alphabet was developed, many of these folk tales were written down. But many were also lost.

A popular literary form is *ki phawar*—poems in couplet form on various subjects set to simple music. Sometimes during the ritual of bringing the bones of a deceased clan or family member to be kept in the clan's ossuary (a container or room in which the bones of dead people are placed), some male members would spontaneously compose and sing a phawar. Sometimes, phawars were composed on the occasion of a group dance, an archery contest or other group activities.

Written Khasi literature began in 1844 with *Ka Gospel of u Matti* (The Gospel of Matthew) by Thomas Jones. In the next few years, a number of Khasi books, all revolving around the Christian religion were published. Several primers and grammar books were also developed, which enabled the teaching of Khasi in schools.

In 1889, *U Nongkitkhubor,* the first Khasi newspaper was established. In 1891, *Kot Bah* was published. This Khasi book contained many stories, records, songs about Khasi history, and many other literary and non-literary forms of writing. This helped establish a clear written form, language and diction for written Khasi.

In 1893, Jeebon Roy Mairom published a book on the indigenous Khasi religion. By 1900, other writers like Rabon Singh Kharsuka, Radhon Singh Kharwanlang, Rev. Morkha Chyne and Hormu Rai Diengdoh had begun to write and publish in Khasi. Since then, Khasi literature has flourished with many writers writing novels, plays and short stories in Khasi. Many missionaries also published Khasi works. Kynpham Sing Nongkynrih, who also writes in English, is among Khasi's more well-known writers today.

Since the Khasis are divided into different clans, spoken Khasi varies from one group to another. But for written Khasi, the language that is spoken and used around Sohra is the version that had been decided as the standard.

Sohra is the Khasi name for the place that the world knows as Cherrapunjee. 'Sohra' was pronounced as 'Cherra' by the British and that's how the place got the name Cherrapunjee. Sohra was for many years considered the wettest place on earth and held the record for the most amount of rainfall in a single month and in a single year. Today, another place close to Sohra—Mawsynram—holds this record.

After the 1972 creation of Meghalaya, many felt that the wide usage of English was posing a threat to the Khasi language. But it appears that the two languages have found a way to co-exist. Khasi is an official language in some Meghalaya districts, and it is widely used in primary and secondary education, radio, television and for religious purposes. Khasi literature is also very vibrant, and it is no longer considered an 'endangered' language. Though some of the spoken forms of Khasi are dying, by and large, the standard form of Khasi seems to be flourishing.

TIMELINE

c.10,000 BCE: The ancestors of the Khasis arrive in the Khasi Hills region.

1823: The British come to the Khasi Hills region.

1844: *Ka Gospel of u Matti* by Rev. Thomas Jones, the first printed Khasi book is published.

1889: *U Nongkitkhubor,* the first Khasi newspaper was established.

1891: *Kot Bah* is published.

1893: Jeebon Roy Mairom's book on the indigenous Khasi religion is published.

1972: The creation of Meghalaya.

As per the latest estimates, there are about a million speakers of Khasi today.[20]

---

[20] *Source:* https://www.ethnologue.com/language/kha/

SINO-TIBETAN LANGUAGES

The speakers of the Sino-Tibetan (sometimes called Tibeto-Burman) family of Indian languages can be found from Ladakh in the north to Arunachal Pradesh in the east.

Some of the widely used Sino-Tibetan languages are:

1. Meeteilon (Manipuri)
2. Ladakhi (Ladakh)
3. Bodo (Assam)
4. Kokborok (Tripura)
5. Lepcha (Sikkim)
6. Bhotia (Sikkim)
7. Mizo (Mizoram)
8. Newari (Nepal)
9. Garo (Meghalaya)
10. Angami Naga (Nagaland)

KOKBOROK

An ancient language reinvented

Have you heard of a language called Kokborok? No?

It is spoken by about a million people in India, allegedly by about 400,000 people in Bangladesh (exact numbers are not available), and is the official language of the state of Tripura. Kokborok belongs to the Sino-Tibetan (sometimes called Tibeto-Burman) family of languages. While its origins are ancient, its path to the modern era has been a meandering one.

Kokborok literature dates back to the first century CE, which means that the language was in use much before that. Historians talk of an ancient text called the *Rajratnakar* originally written in the Koloma script, which was a chronicle of the kings of the region now known as Tripura. Legends say that it was written by one Durlobendra Chontai. The Chontai, in ancient times, was the head priest of the royal dynasties that ruled Tripura and it was his duty to keep the records. It is likely that was how this ancient text came to be written.

> The modern state of Tripura is the third smallest in India
> and completely landlocked. Surrounded almost entirely by
> Bangladesh, its only link to India is the border on its east with
> Assam and Mizoram. Prior to 1947, its capital, Agartala, was only
> about 350 kilometres by road from Kolkata. But since the Partition
> of 1947, the route to Kolkata is more than 1500 kilometres since
> the road has to go around Bangladesh.

The ancient text of *Rajratnakar* has been lost. What we have today are the Bangla and Sanskrit translations and it is through these that scholars came to know about the original text. The date of the Sanskrit translation is not clear, though the names of the translators Sukreswar and Vaneswar are mentioned in the text. The Bangla version dates back to the fourteenth century CE and is known as the *Rajmala*. It is the work of several writers, and it was kept updated with the names of rulers added till the mid-nineteenth century.

Kokborok was formerly known as Tripuri and Tiprakok. These older names are a clear reference to the Twipra kingdom. The word 'Kokborok' came into use only in the twentieth century and has been derived from the word *Kok* meaning 'language' and *Borok* meaning 'human' or 'people', which can also be understood as a reference to the tribal communities of Tripura as Kokborok was the language that was used by all these communities. The language is closely related to the Bodo and Dimasa languages of Assam and to the Garo language, spoken in Meghalaya.

Where did the name 'Tripura' or 'Twipra' originate? One theory holds that the name 'Tripura' comes from

Tripura Sundari, a Hindu goddess. Another theory suggests the Kokborok words *tui* (water) and *pra* (near) as the possible origin of the name. This implies that parts of the ancient Twipra kingdom lay close to the sea. But there is no clear evidence for this.

The *Rajmala* provides a list of kings of the Twipra kingdom dating back several centuries. However, its list of kings prior to the fourteenth century is not entirely reliable since many names appear to be mythical. Based on the evidence available, historians largely concur that the kingdom came into existence around 1400 CE when Maha Manikya founded it after establishing his dominance over the many tribes who populated the area.

Who was Maha Manikya? Originally known as Chhengthung Fa, Maha Manikya probably belonged to the Twipra tribe, which dominated the region. According to the *Rajmala*, Chhengthung Fa fought and won a battle against a ruler of Bengal and took the title 'Maha Manikya'. Incidentally, his queen's name was Tripura Sundari. After the reign of Maha Manikya, which ended in 1431, his successors consolidated the kingdom. At its peak in the sixteenth century (under Dhanya Manikya and Vijaya Manikya II), it covered a considerable area from the Garo Hills of Meghalaya to the Bay of Bengal. At least parts of this kingdom were located by the sea, unlike modern-day Tripura, which is landlocked.

Over the centuries, as the Manikya rulers gained in influence and power, Kokborok as a language seems to have been gradually eclipsed by Bangla, which was given extensive patronage from the days of King Ratna Manikya

(1462–87). During the reign of Bir Chandra Manikya (1862–96), Bangla became the court language. By this time, Kokborok had become largely a spoken tongue, spoken by the *Borok* which consisted of eight major tribal communities—Tripuri, Reang, Jamatia, Noatia, Murasing, Koloi, Rupini and Uchoi.

The Tagore family had close links with the royal family of Tripura from the time of Dwarkanath Tagore, Rabindranath's grandfather. Three important works of Rabindranath Tagore—the plays *Mukuta* (1885) and *Visarjana* (1890) and the novel *Rajarshi* (1885)—were directly influenced by his association with the royal family of Tripura. Tagore later visited the kingdom in 1900. In one of his poems, he writes, 'When the woodlands of Tripura have sent out invitations to their floral feast through their courier of the south wind, I have come as a friend.'

Bir Chandra Manikya was one of the characters in the Bangla novel *Prathom Alo* (First Light) by Sunil Gangopadhyay.

RECENT HISTORY

Since the late nineteenth century, several attempts were made to revive Kokborok and develop it as a written language. In 1900, Radhamohan Thakur published *Kon-Borokma*, a grammar book. He also wrote two other books: *Traipur Kothamala* and *Traipur Bhasabidhan*. Daulot Ahmed, a contemporary of Radhamohan Thakur, wrote a work of grammar jointly with Mohammad Omar. This spurred a Kokborok revival and several other books were published.

After 1947, the revival gained considerable momentum. In 1954, *Kwatal Kothama*, the first Kokborok magazine was published. It was edited by Sudhanya Deb Barma, who also wrote *Hachuk Khurio* (In the Lap of Hills), the first modern Kokborok novel.

Kokborok was declared an official language of the state of Tripura in 1979. Since the 1980s, the language has been taught in schools of Tripura from the primary level to the higher secondary stage. In 1994, a certificate course in Kokborok was started at Tripura University and in 2001, a post-graduate diploma also began. In 2012, Kokborok was introduced in the Bachelor of Arts (BA) programme affiliated with Tripura University and in 2015, a Master of Arts (MA) degree in Kokborok was started.

Historically, Kokborok was written in the Koloma script, of which there are a few traces in some of Tripura's old temples. But after the fourteenth century, the script fell into disuse and was lost. In the nineteenth century, a modified Bangla script began to be used. The Roman script was also advocated by many tribal organizations.

Today, the teaching of the language is done in the Bangla script by the state government but in autonomous tribal areas where local councils run schools, the Roman script is used. Kokborok literature is fairly vibrant and a number of books are published in the language, most of them in the Roman script.

Kokborok will continue to struggle to hold its own against Bangla and English, but the enthusiasm of its speakers is likely to ensure that the language will not disappear anytime soon.

VOWELS (SARITHAI) & DIACRITICS

অ	আ	ই	উ	এ	অঁ		
	া	ি	ু	ে	ৗ	ং	ঁ
ô	ā	i	u	e	aw	ang	añ
[o/ɔ/a]	[a:]	[i]	[u]	[e]	[ɔ]	[ŋ]	[̃]

CONSONANTS (KWTHATHAI)

ক	খ	গ	ঙ	চ	জ	ত	থ
ka	kha	ga	nga	cha	ja	ta	tha
[kɔ]	[kʰɔ]	[gɔ]	[ŋɔ]	[cɔ̃]	[dʒɔ]	[tɔ]	[tʰɔ]

দ	ন	প	ফ	ব	ম	য়	র
da	na	pa	pha	ba	ma	ya	ra
[dɔ]	[nɔ]	[pɔ]	[pʰɔ]	[bɔ]	[mɔ]	[jɔ]	[rɔ]

উা	ল	স	হ
ua	la	sa	ha
[wɔ]	[lɔ]	[sɔ]	[hɔ]

NUMERALS (LEKHATHAI)

১	২	৩	৪	৫	৬	৭	৮
সা	নৈ	থম	ব্রৈ	বা	দোক	স্নি	চার
sa	nwi	tham	brwi	ba	dok	sni	char
1	2	3	4	5	6	7	8

৯	১০
চুকু	চি
chuku	chi
9	10

The modified Bangla alphabet for Kokborok[21]

---

[21] *Source:* https://omniglot.com/writing/kokborok.htm

A a	B b	Ch ch	D d	E e	G g	H h	I i
[a]	[b]	[t͡ʃ]	[d]	[e]	[g]	[h]	[i]
J j	K k	L l	M m	N n	N' n'	Ng ng	O o
[d͡ʒ]	[k]	[l]	[m]	[n]	[ĩ]	[ŋ]	[o]
P p	R r	S s	T t	U u	W w	Y y	
[p]	[r]	[s]	[t]	[u]	[w/ə]	[j]	

The modified Roman alphabet for Kokborok[22]

TIMELINE

1st century CE: The writing of the *Rajratnakar*.

14th century: The writing of the Bangla version of the *Rajratnakar* known as the *Rajmala*.

1900: Radhamohan Thakur published *Kon-Borokma*, a Kokborok grammar book.

1954: *Kwatal Kothama*, the first Kokborok magazine began to be published.

1979: Kokborok declared an official language of the state of Tripura.

1994: A certificate course in Kokborok was started at Tripura University.

2012: Kokborok introduced in the Bachelor of Arts programme.

2015: Master of Arts (MA) degree in Kokborok started.

As per the latest estimates, Kokborok is spoken by about a million people in India.[23]

---

[23] *Source:* https://www.ethnologue.com/language/trp/

MANIPURI

Jewel of the northeast

Manipuri (also called Meeteilon, Meiteilon, Meiteiron, and Meitei) is the most widely spoken Sino-Tibeto (Tibeto-Burman) language in India. Spoken by about 1.8 million people,[24] it is the official language of the state of Manipur, and is also used in Myanmar and Bangladesh. In 1992, it became the first Sino-Tibetan language to receive the scheduled language status in the Indian Constitution.

'Meiteilon' means the 'language of the Meiteis'. The Meiteis are the dominant ethnic group of the state of Manipur, comprising over half the population of the state.

While it is usually Meiteilon which goes by the name 'Manipuri' today, there is another language spoken in the northeast that also is called 'Manipuri'.

Bishnupriya Manipuri, unlike Meiteilon, is an Indo-Aryan language, closely related to Bangla and Assamese but also possesses a

---

[24] *Source:* https://www.ethnologue.com/language/mni/

number of older Meiteilon words in its vocabulary. Most Bishnupriya speakers who number about 100,000 live outside Manipur—in Assam, Tripura and in Bangladesh.[25] Only a small number live in Manipur itself.

HISTORY AND LITERATURE

Scholars speak of an ancient Manipuri song called the *Ougri*, which is supposed to date back to the first century CE. The *Khencho* is a work of poetry that has been dated back to the seventh century CE. Coins from the sixth century CE and a copper plate inscription from the seventh or eighth century CE have also been found, all proof of the language's ancient origins. These establish that Manipuri as a language was in existence even before the *Ougri* was composed. (A general thumb rule used by linguists is that if a literary work can be dated, then it stands to reason that the language was in use even before that.)

Apart from the *Ougri* and *Khencho*, there are many other ancient literary works. There was an ancient tradition of writing manuscripts known as the *puyas*, which were collections of oral literature. One such puya was the *Cheitharol Kumbaba*, the court chronicle of the kings of Manipur starting from 33 CE, and believed to have been first written around the fifteenth century CE. Much of this work is about warfare, internal conflicts and the heroic deeds of the kings of Manipur. But it also provides information about the customs and traditions of the Meitei people. The *Ningthourol Lambuba* is another

---

[25] *Source:* https://www.ethnologue.com/language/bpy/

puya. It is a list of the kings of Manipur along with their activities. It supplemented the *Cheitharol Kumbaba*, providing more details of some of the events mentioned in the *Kumbaba*.

In the eighteenth century, one event altered the history of the state and its people. In 1717, the king Pamheiba proclaimed Vaishnavism to be the state religion. His father, Charairongba, had adopted Vaishnavism in 1704 and even issued coins inscribed with the name of Lord Krishna. Pamheiba, who came to the throne in 1709, initially showed no inclination towards Vaishnavism. But in 1717, he not only adopted the religion but he also went to great lengths to destroy the existing indigenous religious traditions and texts.[26] He adopted the name Garib Nawaz, though some texts also refer to him as Gopal Singh.

During his reign, which lasted until 1751, his subjects were forced to adopt the new religion, their old shrines were destroyed, and their existing rituals and festivals were absorbed into the new religion. Tragically, a number of puyas were destroyed or burnt in order to wipe out any memory of the old religious traditions and customs. Owing to the advent of the new religion, much of the literature that was written began to reflect the new Vaishnavite culture and mythology.

In the 1930s, many puyas resurfaced. But scholars are of the view that many of these were not authentic. Since 1979, the destruction of the puyas has been remembered

---

[26] The old Manipuri religious tradition is today referred to as Sanamahi. It is not clear what it was called earlier. Different scholars offer various other names, none of which can be fully authenticated due to the non-availability of clear evidence.

in an event known as the *Puya Meithaba* (burning of the puya).

Today, many in the Meitei community follow Vaishnavite traditions though the old religious traditions also continue to be part of Meitei life. There is also a Meitei Muslim community known as the Pangals.

SCRIPT

The old Manipuri script was known as the Kanglei or the Kok Sam Lei script. The earliest examples date back to coins issued during the era of King Ura Konthouba (568–653 CE). A copper plate Meitei inscription from the reign of King Khongtekcha (c. 721 CE) was discovered by a scholar named Yumjao from Phayeng village to the east of Imphal in 1935. It is one of the earliest known written records of Meitei literature.

Between the early eighteenth and the middle of the twentieth century, the Manipuri language was written using the Bangla alphabet. During the 1940s and 1950s, Manipuri scholars began campaigning to bring back the old Manipuri script. In the 1970s, scholars agreed on a new modernized version of the alphabet, which contained a number of additional letters to represent sounds that were not present in the language when the script was first developed. The current Manipuri script is a reconstruction of the ancient Manipuri script and is known as Mayek.

Though the script was approved for official use by 1980, it took many years for it to become popular. According to news reports, the Mayek script was only fully adopted by all Manipuri-language newspapers in early 2023.

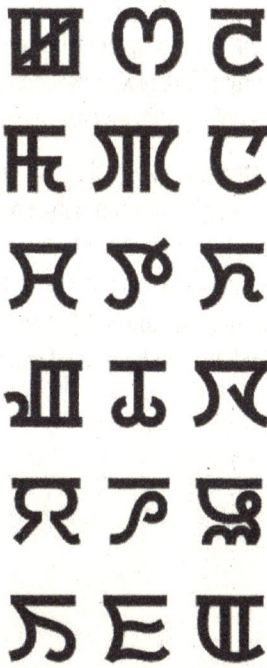

The Mayek script[27]

Today, Manipuri is of course used widely in the state. It is also studied outside the state by scholars who wish to understand the Manipuri dance form. The Manipuri dance, also referred to as the Manipuri Raas Leela, is one of the eight classical dance forms of India. This dance form is largely based on Vaishnaivite traditions and is entirely religious. The challenges to its widespread use are from English and Hindi and like many other languages, it is an uphill struggle to continue to remain relevant.

_____

[27] *Source:* http://wwwmymanipur.blogspot.com/2013/11/meitei-mayek.html

The origins of the game of polo, as we know it today, go back to the ancient Manipuri game of *Sangol Kangjei*. The *Cheitharol Kumbaba* gives an account of a polo match as early as 33 CE.

It was in the late eighteenth century that the British noticed the princes of Manipur playing a game on horseback that involved hitting a ball with a mallet. Intrigued, they later took to the game themselves before introducing it in England in the mid-1800s. In 1901, the then viceroy of India, Lord Curzon, witnessed a game at the Imphal Polo Ground and wrote about it in his book, *A Viceroy's Notebook*.

TIMELINE

- 1st century CE: Likely date of the *Ougri*.

  - 6th century: Likely date of coins. Earliest evidence of the old Manipuri script, known as the *Kanglei* or the *Kok Sam Lei* script in coins.

- 7th century: Likely date of the *Khencho*. A copper plate inscription dating back to this time has also been found.

  - 15th century: The *Cheitharol Kumbaba*, the court chronicle of the kings of Manipur was likely written.

- 1717: Pamheiba proclaimed Vaishnavism to be the state religion.

  - 1980: Mayek script approved for official use.

- 1992: Manipuri (Meiteilon) became the first Sino-Tibetan language to receive the sheduled language status in the Indian Constitution.

As per the latest estimates, Manipuri is spoken by about 1.8 million people.[28]

---

[28] *Source:* https://www.ethnologue.com/language/mni/

THE STORY OF NAGAMESE

Nagamese has been, for close to a century and a half, the lingua franca of the people of Nagaland and parts of Assam. It is a hybrid of Naga languages, all of which belong to the Sino-Tibetan family, and Assamese, an Indo-Aryan language. Nagamese has also borrowed words from Hindi and English and a few from Bangla. It occupies a distinct space in the region and plays a unique role serving as a connector between the various Naga tribes. It also facilitates communication between the Nagas and the Assamese.

THE EARLY HISTORY OF THE NAGAS

The precise origin and pre-history of the Naga people is something historians and anthropologists are still unable to authoritatively state. Vedic references to the Kiratas and their sub-tribe, the Nagas, have been understood to refer to the progenitors of modern-day Nagas. The Kiratas referred to the hill-people from East India. The story of Uloopi, the Naga princess who married Arjun on his sojourn to eastern India, is another tale that is often cited as possible evidence of the early Nagas.

The historical view is that Tibeto-Burman tribes came through Burma and entered the northeastern region around 1000 BCE. When they did so, they perhaps displaced Austro-Asiatic populations that had settled there between 2500 and 2000 BCE. The Khasis were pushed into the hills of Meghalaya and the Tibeto-Burmans settled in Assam and in the Brahmaputra valley. The tribes now identified as Naga probably moved into Nagaland after the initial waves of migration had already entered Assam. Various sources also make mention that Ptolemy in his *Geographia*, written around 150 CE refers to the 'Nagalogae' of India, but it is difficult to fathom whom he is referring to, as he says little beyond that. Then for several centuries, the Nagas largely disappeared from the available historical records. There is no mention of the Nagas in the records of the kingdom of Kamarupa, which flourished between the fourth and twelfth centuries in present-day Assam.

In 1228, the Ahoms under Sukaphaa entered the Brahmaputra valley through Arunachal Pradesh and founded a kingdom. The Ahoms were originally from Yunnan in China and were Tai people, a linguistic community spread across southeast Asia, China and northeastern India. Over the next few centuries, the Ahoms adopted Hindu practices and began to use Assamese. Since Assamese is an Indo-Aryan language, it is connected to Sanskrit, but more specifically, it is descended from the Magadhi Prakrit of eastern India and had already been in use before the arrival of the Ahoms.

Ahom *buranjis* (chronicles) record a number of interactions that the Ahoms had with the Nagas. The initial encounters were acrimonious and the Nagas appear to have rebelled against the Ahoms by raiding the plains and plundering the produce. The buranjis also refer to the expeditions sent to curb the Nagas and the capture of salt wells in Naga territory by the Ahoms. In the centuries that followed, until the collapse of the Ahom kingdom in 1826 and its incorporation into British India, the Ahoms and Nagas clashed from time to time, but also, for long stretches of time, lived in tentative peace.

British rule in Assam and Nagaland post-1826 altered the existing equations between the Ahoms and the Nagas and also among the Nagas themselves. In the initial part of their rule, the British did not interfere with the Nagas. But, when the Nagas continued to raid the plain regions which were now in British hands, a police station was established in the Nagaland region in 1866 to keep a watch on the region. By 1878 the British had brutally suppressed Naga uprisings against their rule and taken over the administration.

THE LANGUAGE SITUATION

There are about twenty-three Naga languages, all mutually unintelligible. While the tribes did share some cultural similarities and lived in close proximity, there was no common language. Centuries of contact between the Nagas and Assamese had ensured that a few Nagas from the many tribes had some knowledge of Assamese. Owing to the limited contact that the Nagas and Ahoms had, this was sufficient. But the growth of tea plantations in Assam, the establishment of a military garrison at Kohima, the coming of the missionaries into Nagaland, the arrival of the British meant that the Naga tribes had to interact with each other and the Assamese far more than in the past. It was in such a situation that a new language, later to be called Nagamese, emerged, and soon began to be used widely. There is some evidence, though, that the tongue seemed to have already emerged in pre-British times.

THE GROWTH OF NAGAMESE

Lt. Bigges's *Tour Diary* (1841) provides details of the first British expedition into Nagaland, in 1839. Bigges mentions the existence of a language that is clearly Nagamese. It is likely that the British observed that a tongue that sounded something like Assamese was already in use in the Naga areas.

In his *Linguistic Survey of India* (published between 1903 and 1928—the section on Naga languages was published in 1904), G.A. Grierson talks of a language resembling Assamese and mixed with the Naga languages as being spoken in parts of Assam (Nagaland was then part of undivided Assam). The research for this section dealing with the Naga languages was done in the 1890s and it seems that Nagamese was already in wide use by then.

The anthropologists who flocked to Nagaland in British times also mention the presence among the Nagas of a language clearly identifiable as Nagamese. J.H. Hutton's work on the Angami Nagas published in 1921 talks of 'broken Assamese' being spoken in the Naga Hills. Christoph von Fürer Haimendorf, in his work on the Nagas published in 1939, again mentions that many people including children spoke fluent Nagamese, which he terms 'the lingua franca of (the) entire Naga Hills'.

Post-independence, the Naga Hills were part of Assam till the state of Nagaland was formally created on 1 December 1963. English was proclaimed the official language of the new state though Nagamese continued as the lingua franca. It began to be used on the floor of the legislative assembly since it was the only language that was spoken and understood by all. It also began to be used in radio broadcasts and for church services. Inter-tribal marriages resulted in further use of Nagamese. In 2013, a Nagamese newspaper (in the Roman script) *Nagamese Khobor* was launched and continues to run.

However, the wide use of Nagamese has not given the language a respectable status in the eyes of the Nagas. In 2015, the central government announced its intention to give official recognition to Nagamese (this has not yet been done). But many organizations opposed this move stating that Nagamese wasn't a Naga language or a true symbol of Naga identity. The Naga Students Federation termed Nagamese a 'market language' and a language with 'no origin'. Others said that this would act against Naga 'intellectual interests' and wanted to continue with English till the Nagas were able to resolve this issue among themselves.

Except for a small group of people of inter-tribal marriages, Nagamese is not a mother tongue for most Nagas.

In 1989, only about 30,000 people listed Nagamese as their mother tongue. The latest estimates are unavailable. The population of Nagaland is about two million and so the number of people claiming Nagamese as a mother tongue is unlikely to be a very big number.

The future of Nagamese is a wide open one. Its extensive use in the region and its role as a lingua franca negates the possibility of it falling into disuse. But it is not a very respected tongue, and that perception is unlikely to change anytime soon.

INDO-ARYAN LANGUAGES

In terms of number of speakers, the Indo-Aryan family is the largest of the Indian language families. About seventy-five per cent of India's population speak a language belonging to this family. Its speakers are also the majority in Pakistan, Nepal, Bangladesh and Sri Lanka. There are more than 200 Indo-Aryan languages. Some like Hindi-Urdu, Marathi, Bangla, Gujarati and Punjabi have tens of millions of speakers.

All modern Indo-Aryan languages trace their origins back to Sanskrit. From Sanskrit, the road to modern Indo-Aryan languages meandered through two other destinations: Prakrit and Apabhramsa, before finally settling down around 1000–1100 CE as early forms of the various modern Indo-Aryan languages spoken today.

Some other Indo-Aryan languages are:

1. Assamese
2. Konkani
3. Sinhalese
4. Nepali
5. Dogri
6. Maithili

MARATHI
Bridging the north-south divide

One of the more unusual places where Marathi is spoken is in the state of Israel. Many Jews from coastal Maharashtra, known as the Bene Israel (Children of Israel), migrated to Israel after 1948 and have kept the language alive in their communities and gatherings in their adopted home.

Legend has it that the Bene Israel washed up on the coast near Mumbai, due to a shipwreck, in the first or second century CE and chose to settle there. In time, they began dressing like the locals, speaking like them, even as they preserved their distinct religious customs and traditions. The Bene Israeli settlement took place at a time when Marathi itself had not yet taken shape.

The story of Marathi language begins with the Naneghat inscription in the first century BCE, at the time of the Satavahana dynasty. This inscription in the Brahmi script is in a form of Prakrit, which is now known as Maharashtri Prakrit. Marathi is one of the languages that evolved from Maharashtri Prakrit (another is Konkani).

The Satavahanas, also known as the Andhras, which perhaps indicates their place of origin, ruled from Prathisthana (modern-day Paithan in Aurangabad district). That they chose to use Maharashtri Prakrit for their inscriptions suggests that they had probably adopted the language of the people of the region, though their origins lay elsewhere.

Maharashtri Prakrit evolved over the course of the next few centuries into Marathi. The earliest identifiably Marathi text is a copper-plate inscription dated to 739 CE. By the eleventh or twelfth century CE, Marathi appears to have become a widely used language in the region that we now know as Maharashtra.

Under the Yadava dynasty, who ruled from their capital, Devagiri (near Aurangabad) from around 1150 CE, Marathi came into prominence. Initially, the dynasty seems to have used Kannada, since the Yadavas likely hailed from the region now known as Karnataka. But since they were ruling a region that had Marathi speakers, over time, especially from the fourteenth century, the rulers began to use more and more Marathi. In an inscription from c.1311, they even refer to themselves as 'Marathe'.

The Yadava rule was also the time when Marathi literature evolved. The earliest extant Marathi work of literature was devotional poetry composed by holy men belonging to the Mahanubhav and Warkari sects. Dnyaneshwar (1275–96) was the first Marathi writer whose work *Dnyaneshwari* gained considerable popularity.

The location of present-day Maharashtra is such that it has absorbed influences from both south and north India. While the early ruling dynasties of the region (like the Satavahanas and Yadavas) were from southern India, later the region came under the influence of whoever was ruling Delhi. In addition, there were formidable rulers who hailed from the Marathi-speaking region itself. Marathi reflects all these influences.

THE MARATHAS

Between the mid-seventeenth and early nineteenth century, the Marathas became a prominent power, initially in Maharashtra, but gradually they also came to control large parts of northern and southern India. With their enhanced political influence, their language also grew in importance.

The best known Maratha king is Chhatrapati Shivaji (1630–80). His grandfather, Maloji and his brother, Vithoji, abandoned farming to become warriors in the administration of the Ahmednagar Sultan and scripted the rise of the family fortunes. The brothers fought a number of campaigns under the command of the famous Abyssinian general, Malik Ambar, and honed their skills in the art of warfare. Malik Ambar was a shrewd tactician and had even humbled the Mughal army. In time, Maloji's son, Shahaji, also served as an army commander and administrator. Shivaji of course struck a bold new path by establishing his own kingdom by defying the Mughals.

After many years of defying the Mughal emperor, Aurangzeb, Shivaji ascended the throne in 1674 and assumed the title of Chhatrapati. Marathi became the official language and began to be used in official documents. Shivaji tasked one of his officials with finding Sanskrit equivalents for the many Arabic and Persian words to use in administration.

After Shivaji's time, after some initial setbacks, Maratha power spread, especially during the time of Shahu I (1682–1749), Shivaji's grandson. This was largely due to the efforts of the Peshwas, the prime ministers appointed by Shahu I. During the time of Peshwa Bajirao I (1700–40), Maratha rule extended from parts of Tamil Nadu up to Peshawar and from Maharashtra to Bengal.

Marathi spread over the entire geographical region that the Marathas controlled.

> The existence of a unique brand of Marathi, popularly called Thanjavur Marathi, is evidence of how Marathi bridges the north-south divide. Marathi speakers came to the Thanjavur region in Tamil Nadu along with Venkoji (or Vyankoji, also sometimes known as Ekoji), Shivaji's half-brother, in the late 1600s. There have been Marathi speakers there ever since. Until the middle of the nineteenth century, Thanjavur also had a king who was a Marathi speaker.
>
> Thanjavur Marathi is an older form of Marathi—as in, it retains similarities with eighteenth-century Marathi, while modern-day Marathi in Maharashtra has evolved—which developed in isolation from other Marathi-speaking regions and also has some Tamil influence.

Maratha political influence waned after their defeat by the Afghan marauder, Ahmed Shah Abdali, at the Third Battle of Panipat in 1761 and came to an end by 1818 when the British defeated them.

However, during the eighteenth century, many Maratha chieftains had established princely kingdoms throughout the Maratha sphere of influence and Marathi found a home in all of them. Thanjavur in Tamil Nadu, Sandur in Karnataka, Baroda in Gujarat, Indore, Dewas and Gwalior in Madhya Pradesh and Jhansi in Uttar Pradesh (where Rani Lakshmibai, the heroine of the first war of Indian independence in 1857, who was of Maratha origin, ruled) were some of these kingdoms. Several Marathi speakers made a home in these kingdoms and established the language in these areas.

Many Maratha kingdoms continued to have rulers of Maratha origin till 1947, after which they were merged into various Indian states.

THE SAMYUKTA MAHARASHTRA MOVEMENT

During the freedom struggle, the Congress had stated that its goal was to create linguistic states once India had attained independence. Many linguistic organizations were created during the freedom struggle to rally support for this idea. Marathi was no exception.

But after 1947, there was a lot of reluctance to implement the idea of linguistic states. The creation of Pakistan had created a sense of fear in the political leadership about the possibility of further splits in the country, this time on linguistic lines.

During the 1950s, the Samyukta Maharashtra movement was important in shaping a distinct Maharashtrian identity and creating a Marathi-speaking state within India. The movement was an attempt to pressurize the central government to integrate all the Marathi speaking regions into one state with Bombay as its capital.

After a lot of delays and persuasion, in 1956, the bilingual Bombay State was created. This state comprised of what is today Gujarat and Maharashtra and integrated all Gujarati and Marathi speakers into a single state. The demand for an exclusive Marathi-speaking state was not agreed to. The reason for doing so was partly because both linguistic groups had laid claim to Bombay, India's commercial capital. For proponents of a united Maharashtra, it was unthinkable that Bombay would not form part of the state.

Over the next few years, the Samyukta Maharashtra movement relentlessly argued its case and led a number of protests for the creation of Maharashtra. Ultimately in 1960, Maharashtra came into being with Bombay as the capital.

THE SCRIPT

The script used to write Marathi is known as Balbodh, which is similar to Devanagari, but has an extra letter to accommodate Marathi sounds. In the past, besides Balbodh, Marathi was also written in the Modi script. From around the thirteenth century till the middle of the twentieth century, while Balbodh was used for literature, Modi was the preferred script for administration and business documents. Scholars believe that this was on account of the fact that Modi reduced the need for the pen to be lifted from the paper while writing and thus enabled swift writing.

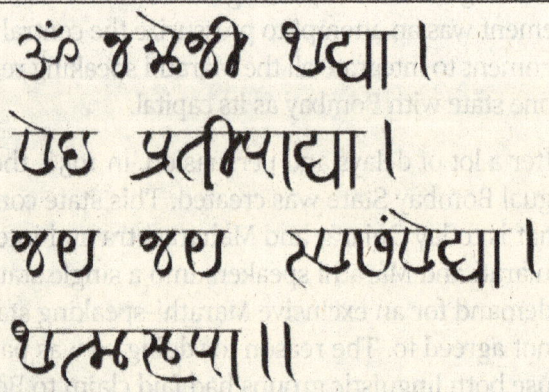

A verse of *Dnyaneshwari* in Modi script.[29]

---

[29] Note its similarity to Devanagari. *Source:* https://en.wikipedia.org/wiki/Modi_script#/media/File:Dnyaneshwari_Verse_In_Modi_Script.png

Modi is derived from the Marathi word *modane*, which means 'to bend or break'. The script is believed to have evolved from broken Devanagari letters and hence the name. When documents began to be printed in Marathi in the nineteenth century, Balbodh became the preferred script. Almost no printing was done in Modi. Almost all the extant Modi manuscripts are handwritten. The Saraswati Mahal

VOWELS

अ आ इ ई उ ऊ
ए ऐ ओ औ अं अः

CONSONANTS

क ख ग घ ङ

च छ ज झ ञ

ट ठ ड ढ ण

त थ द ध न

प फ ब भ म

य र ल व श

ष स ह ळ क्ष ज्ञ

The Balbodh script is almost entirely similar to Devanagari.
The ळ is a modification.[30]

[30] ळ is a deeper way of saying 'la' with the tongue curving inwards. There is no equivalent sound in English to try and convey its exact pronunciation.

Library in Thanjavur is a repository of Marathi manuscripts written in Modi. The usage of Modi came to an end by around 1950 and Marathi only uses the Balbodh script today.

Konkani, spoken all along the Malabar and Konkan coasts by the Arabian Sea, is closely related to Marathi. Konkani is one of Goa's official languages and it is the predominant language of the state. Konkani speakers are found in Karnataka and Kerala too. Scholars believe that Konkani acquired a distinct and separate identity around 1000 CE. In a poem by the Marathi poet Namdev (1270–1350), he refers to 'Konkani cowgirls'. He also wrote a Konkani verse for the Konkani milkmaid and a separate verse for the Marathi milkmaid.

It is believed that Konkani speakers migrated to Kerala from the twelfth century, and to the Mangalore region in Karnataka in the fifteenth and sixteenth centuries. Since Konkani speakers live all along the west coast in different linguistic zones (Kannada, Malayalam and Marathi), Konkani came to be written in five scripts: Devanagari, Kannada, Malayalam, Roman and Perso-Arabic (by Konkani-speaking Navayath Muslims).

Devanagari is now the predominant script of Konkani though the Roman script continues to be used by the Church. The Kannada script is used in Karnataka. The usage of the Perso-Arabic script has reduced considerably and the usage of Malayalam script by Konkanis in Kerala has been replaced by Devanagari.

Marathi is today the official language of Maharashtra. It is also used in Goa, parts of northern Karnataka and Dadra and Nagar Haveli. It continues to be in some use in the former Maratha-ruled princely kingdoms of southern, central and northern India.

Modern Marathi literature has been extremely influential in the Indian literary universe and of special importance in the late twentieth century. *Sakharam Binder* and *Ghasiram Kotwal* are two of playwright Vijay Tendulkar's most influential plays. They were translated into several languages and performed widely, besides being greatly popular in Maharashtra. The Dalit literary movement in Marathi, which was sparked by the works of Namdeo Dhasal, Baburao Bagul, Daya Pawar and many others, brought to the fore a new literary sensibility which was unlike anything seen before.

Marathi cinema has always been dwarfed by the overarching presence of Hindi cinema, since both these industries were centred in Mumbai. Many Marathi actors and filmmakers chose to work in the more lucrative Hindi film industry. But in recent years, some extremely interesting films have been made in Marathi and it has emerged into the limelight. *Harishchandrachi Factory* (2009) was a depiction of the struggles of Dadasaheb Phalke, the iconic Indian filmmaker who made *Raja Harishchandra* (1913), the first full-length Indian feature film. *Sairat* (2016) was another extremely popular Marathi film which was later remade in other Indian languages.

TIMELINE

1st century BCE: Likely date of the Naneghat inscription in Maharashtri Prakrit

739 CE: The earliest identifiably Marathi copper plate inscription.

1200s: Usage of Marathi by the Yadavas.

Post-1650: Marathi greatly encouraged by the Marathas as their territories grew.

1956–60: The Samyukta Maharashtra movement.

1960: The state of Maharashtra created.

As per the latest estimates, about eighty-three million people speak Marathi as their first language.[31]

---

[31] *Source:* https://www.ethnologue.com/language/mar/

PUNJABI
Uniting India and Pakistan

In Jerusalem, there stands a structure with a Punjabi connection that is more than 800 years old. The Farid Sarai is a shrine and a lodge that commemorates the visit of the Sufi saint, Baba Farid to the city en route to Mecca.

Baba Farid (1173–1266) belonged to the Chishti order of Sufis and was among the first known Punjabi poets. He composed hundreds of poems, many of which have been included in the *Guru Granth Sahib*, the sacred text of Sikhism. Punjabi was definitely in use as a spoken language at least for a few hundred years before Baba Farid. But no history of the language can begin without invoking his name.

Baba Farid was born in Multan, in modern-day West Punjab, Pakistan. Revered by Muslims, Hindus and Sikhs alike, Baba Farid's biggest contribution to Punjabi was that he developed the language for literary use. In the past, Sanskrit, Persian and Arabic had been the language of literature in Punjab. But Baba Farid's usage of Punjabi inspired a more extensive use of the language. The city of Faridkot in East Punjab, India bears his name.

Punjabi, the name of the language, is derived from the word 'Punjab', today the name of a state in both India and Pakistan and historically, a region in the Indian subcontinent. Punjab is derived from the Persian word 'Panj-Ab', meaning 'five waters', which refers to the five rivers (Ravi, Satluj, Chenab, Beas and Jhelum) that flow through the region. All the five rivers are tributaries of the river Indus.

The beginnings of Punjabi are traced to around the eighth or ninth century CE. Punjabi developed from Prakrit and Apabhramsa, specifically from Shauraseni Prakrit. Some scholars believe that Paishachi Prakrit also influenced the development of the language. The earliest writings that contain elements of Punjabi in them are the writings of the Nath Yogis, a Shaivite sect with centres throughout the subcontinent, including in Punjab. Scholars have dated the earliest writings of the Nath Yogis to the ninth century CE. The work of Baba Farid a couple of hundred years later established the language as a literary one.

Around the fifteenth century, a number of literary works were written in Punjabi which spurred the development of the language. The writings of Guru Nanak (1469–1439), the founder of Sikhism and the first guru of the Sikhs, were highly influential. Nanak chose to write in Punjabi instead of Sanskrit or Persian and several of his verses were later included in the *Guru Granth Sahib*. The *Janamsakhis*, which were accounts of Nanak's life and teachings, were also written in Punjabi and are some of the earliest prose writings in the language. Many of the Sikh gurus who followed Nanak also wrote in Punjabi.

The writings of Guru Angad, Guru Amar Das, Guru Ram Das, Guru Arjan Dev and Guru Tegh Bahadur are all in the *Granth Sahib*.

> The central text of Sikhism, the *Guru Granth Sahib*, is an important text in Punjabi literature. It contains the writings of about thirty-six poets, including six Sikh gurus. It was compiled by Guru Arjan Dev in 1604 CE at Amritsar. While many of the writings are in Punjabi, it also contains texts in Braj, Sanskrit and Persian. When the text was first compiled, the Gurmukhi script was used throughout.

Another important early Punjabi writer was Shah Hussain (1538–99), who wrote as Madho Lal Hussain, the name incorporating a reference to Madho Lal, his disciple and possibly lover. Shah Hussain's poetry is sung to this day and his tomb in Lahore is very popular with pilgrims who celebrate his birth anniversary every year with great fervour.

An important tradition in medieval Punjabi literature is the *qissa*, a tradition of oral storytelling and singing. It celebrates love, loyalty, honour and mourns sacrifice and betrayal. The most famous ones narrate the tales of star-crossed lovers whom the world conspires to separate and keep apart. *Heer-Ranjha* by Waris Shah, *Sohni Mahiwal* by Fazal Shah, *Mirza Sahiba* by Hafiz Barkhudar and *Sassi Punnun* by Hashim Shah are other famous qissas. Bulleh Shah (1680–1757) was another well-known Punjabi writer whose *kafi* form of poetry is extremely popular. The kafi is a spiritual poetry form that brings together Sufi and Bhakti ideas.

In the history of Punjab, Maharaja Ranjit Singh (1780–1839) figures prominently. He established a powerful empire in the early nineteenth century with its capital at Lahore. He was instrumental in melding the three communities—Hindu, Muslim and Sikh—into a united Punjabi identity with a sense of pride and distinction. The reason for his importance in the history of the language is that this identity was fostered by the use of the common tongue.

SCRIPTS

In East Punjab, Punjabi is written in the Gurmukhi script. It appears that the script was modelled on Landa, an existing script, which was earlier used for Punjabi. It is also similar to the Sharda script and also has some similarities to Devanagari, all of which trace their origin to Brahmi. According to Sikh tradition, the Gurmukhi script was created by Guru Angad (1504–52), the second guru of the Sikhs. Scholars, however, believe that his role lay in popularizing and standardizing the script since there is evidence that the script was in existence earlier.

In West Punjab, the Shahmukhi script is used. It is identical to the Urdu script, except that Shahmukhi has incorporated a few adjustments to capture the sounds of Punjabi. The usage of Shahmukhi probably began during the Mughal period when Persian began to be used a great deal in the region.

In the past, Devanagari and Mahajani were also used to write Punjabi, the latter mainly by the business community. These are no longer used.

The word 'Punjabi' written in Gurmukhi, Devanagari and Shahmukhi

ੳ	ਅ	ੲ	ਸ	ਹ
ਕ	ਖ	ਗ	ਘ	ਙ
ਚ	ਛ	ਜ	ਝ	ਞ
ਟ	ਠ	ਡ	ਢ	ਣ
ਤ	ਥ	ਦ	ਧ	ਨ
ਪ	ਫ	ਬ	ਭ	ਮ
ਯ	ਰ	ਲ	ਵ	ੜ

The Gurmukhi script

The Shahmukhi script

PUNJABI AFTER 1947

The 1947 partition of Punjab has played an important role in the subsequent history of the language. The loss of Lahore, the cultural centre of united Punjab, was a huge blow to Punjabis in India.

In Pakistan, while Punjabi is the most widely spoken language, used by about forty per cent of the population (about eighty million people), the government has actively promoted Urdu as the national language, thereby relegating Punjabi (and other regional languages like Pashto, Sindhi and Baloch) to a lesser position. In West Punjab, this has greatly derailed the development of the language. Since independence, the language has not been formally taught in schools and colleges. Most writers too prefer to write in Urdu, since there is greater state patronage. In recent years, though, Punjabi in Pakistan has undergone something of a revival and many writers are writing in the language. The growth of social media has given language activists another tool to popularize the language. In 2021, Punjabi language activists agitated for Punjabi to be taught in schools and for Punjabi to be allowed in the legislatures.

Two languages closely related to Punjabi are Seraiki (also spelt as Saraiki and Siraiki) and Hindko, both largely spoken in Pakistan. Seraiki is spoken in southern West Punjab and northern Sindh in Pakistan and by some migrants from these regions who came to India after Partition. Some scholars believe that Seraiki is closer to Sindhi in some respects, but Seraiki is intelligible to Punjabi speakers too. In recent years, demands have been made by Seraiki speakers for a separate province in Pakistan.

> Hindko has also borrowed many words from Pashto, the language
> of Afghanistan and the Khyber Pakhtunkhwa province in Pakistan.
> It is spoken by close to four million people in Pakistan in northern
> West Punjab and in the Khyber Pakhtunkhwa province. There are a
> substantial number of speakers of Hindko in cities like Peshawar,
> Nowshera, Swabi and Kohat, all in Khyber-Pakhtunkhwa.

In India, Punjabi is spoken by about thirty million
people. It is the official language of Punjab, and the
additional official language of Haryana and Delhi.

After independence, despite many demands, a separate
Punjabi-speaking state in India was not created for a
long time. For close to two decades after independence,
Punjab in India was a bilingual province with both Hindi
and Punjabi speakers. Punjabi was branded the 'language
of the Sikhs' and in the early 1960s, some organizations
ran a campaign to encourage Punjabi-speaking Hindus to
declare Hindi their mother tongue to prevent the creation
of a Punjabi-speaking Punjab.

Eventually, after considerable protests, present-day
Punjab was created in 1966 by dividing Punjab province
into two states—Punjab, where Punjabi is the majority
language, and Haryana, a separate Hindi-speaking
state. The capital city, Chandigarh, which had been
specially created after 1947 to compensate for the loss
of Lahore, was declared a union territory and was to
be the shared capital of both states. This continues till
today and is a sore point with many Punjabis. This,
along with a number of other political and economic
issues, spawned the separatist Khalistan movement

in the 1980s which resulted in many deaths and the disruption of everyday life. This significantly affected Punjabi cultural life, especially cinema, which ground to a halt by the mid-1980s.

Prior to independence, Lahore was an important centre for the production of Hindi and Punjabi films. After the loss of Lahore to Pakistan, many Punjabi actors, writers and filmmakers shifted to Mumbai and opted to work in the more remunerative Hindi film industry. While a number of Punjabi films were produced, it was small compared to Hindi. By the mid-1980s, owing to political troubles, Punjabi films had almost died out.

Since 2000, the Punjabi film industry has witnessed a revival. While many Punjabi films are potboilers in the crime and comedy genres, the work of Gurvinder Singh (*Anhe Ghore Da Daan*, *Chauthi Koot* and *Adh Chanani Raat*) has received great critical acclaim. Uniquely, owing to its considerable diaspora, many Punjabi films are almost entirely shot abroad and document the struggles of the many Punjabi immigrants in the west, especially in the UK and Canada. Punjabi web series (*CAT* and *Kohra*, for instance) are also beginning to find a national audience with their captivating plots and themes.

Punjabi's greatest cultural import in recent times has been its popular music. Dance music with popular Punjabi tunes and rhythms, largely synonymous with bhangra, the folk dance of Punjab, and mixed with western instruments and sounds have proved to be a hit worldwide. Artistes like Punjabi MC, Jazzy B, Malkit Singh, Harbhajan Mann and many others have huge followings in India, the UK and Canada. Besides dance music, singers like Nusrat Fateh Ali Khan, Rahat Fateh Ali Khan, the Nooran sisters and many others have also popularized Punjabi Sufi music, which has now found an audience far beyond Punjab and the Punjabi diaspora.

Punjabi literature is also thriving with a number of writers and poets actively writing in and promoting the language, in India, Pakistan and in the UK and Canada. The UK and Canada also have radio and television channels in Punjabi. The works of Gurdial Singh, Dalip Kaur Tiwana, Surjit Patar, Amarjit Chandan and many others are extremely popular. Amrita Pritam was a giant of twentieth-century Punjabi literature whose novels, short stories and poetry, many of them with feminist themes, enjoy cult-like status. Another extremely popular writer was Shiv Kumar Batalvi, who died young. Nainsukh and Mahmood Awan are popular Pakistani writers of Punjabi. An issue unique to Punjabi is the lack of a common script in India and Pakistan, which has prevented Punjabis from both sides being able to read each other's literature.[32]

In India, Punjabi in recent times has to some extent struggled to hold its own against Hindi and English. Immigration from Punjab, both to other states in India as well as the West has resulted in Punjabi's popularity diminishing, especially among the younger generation.

---

[32] This is in contrast with West Bengal and Bangladesh, which though separate, are able to participate in each other's cultural and literary activities due to the common script for Bangla which they share.

TIMELINE

9th century CE: Nath yogis used elements of Punjabi in their writings.

1200s: Baba Farid used the language for his poetry.

1450 onwards: A number of writers, including Sikh gurus, used the language for their writings. Gurmukhi script popularized by Guru Angad.

1604: Guru Arjun Dev compiled the *Guru Granth Sahib*.

1800–1839: Reign of Maharaja Ranjit Singh.

1947: Partition of Punjab into East and West.

1966: The Punjab state created in India.

In Pakistan, Punjabi is the most widely spoken language, used by about forty per cent of the population—about eighty million people.[33] In India, Punjabi is spoken by about thirty million people.[34]

---

[33] 'CCI defers approval of census results until elections', Khaleeq Kiani, 28 May 2018, https://www.dawn.com/news/1410447

[34] 'Abstract of Speakers' Strength of Languages and Mother Tongues – 2011', https://web.archive.org/web/20220201042328/https://www.censusindia.gov.in/2011Census/Language-2011/Statement-1.pdf

HINDI

A language with an attitude

When Grierson was compiling the Linguistic Survey of India in the 1890s, he stated that the language of 'the Gangetic Valley between Bengal and the Punjab' was 'Hindi with its numerous dialects'. In 1869, when Sir Syed Ahmad Khan, educationist and writer, travelled across India, he said that from 'Allahabad to Bombay', he could use Urdu everywhere and people easily understood it.

In the 1950s, the American linguist Gumperz spent some time in Uttar Pradesh. In one village, where he was conducting his research, the story goes that he happened to speak to a Hindu family who complimented him on his Hindi. A few minutes later, he spoke to a Muslim family who complimented him on his Urdu. Gumperz was speaking exactly the same language with both families. It hadn't been any different in the nineteenth century when Grierson and Khan made their statements.

These stories illustrate how the history of Hindi is rather more complicated than that of many other languages. Today, Hindi and Urdu are languages people think of as separate and distinct, with separate scripts. But the history of these languages is intertwined and the history of one is to a great extent the history of the other. There are scholars who consider Hindi-Urdu broadly one language. They think of it as a spectrum with 'Hindi' at one end with lots of Sanskrit and 'Urdu' at another with lots of Persian. In the centre lies Hindi and Urdu without the quotes, which are Sanskrit and Persian in equal measure. Some call it Hindi and some Urdu, though they are broadly the same.

The origins of the languages themselves are rather straightforward—all Indo-Aryan languages trace their history to Sanskrit through Prakrit and Apabhramsa. Hindi-Urdu are no different. But, due to historical circumstances, Persian, Turkish and Arabic too have played a part in the development of these languages. Often, their history is a matter of debate and disagreement since religion and political developments in the last two hundred years have also influenced the views and thinking of scholars in these languages.

WHAT'S IN A NAME?

For a long time, the word 'Hindustani' was used when talking about the history of Hindi and Urdu. While scholars do have a way to distinguish Hindi, Urdu and Hindustani from each other, it is difficult to do so very precisely. As a thumb rule, 'Hindi' is the language that consists of many more words of Sanskritic origin while 'Urdu' consists of many more words of Persian origin. 'Hindustani' is said to consist of an equal number of words of Sanskrit and Persian origin. When Hindi or Urdu are used in official contexts by government departments in India or Pakistan, the usage tends to be stricter, with preference given to words of Sanskrit or Persian origin (if there are options), depending on where the language is being used. In the spoken language, however, such deliberate choices are seldom made, and the rules are applied very loosely. The speakers of one can, with no or very little effort, understand the other.

> The best example of Hindustani can be found in what we call the 'Hindi' film industry centred in Mumbai, which, if we were to be very exact about nomenclature, uses Hindustani as its language, with words of both Persian and Sanskrit origin. While Hindi films are extremely popular in India, they are equally popular in Pakistan. There is no barrier for Urdu-speaking Pakistanis to understanding the 'Hindi' that is used in the films.
>
> Similarly, Pakistani television serials, all using Urdu, are extremely popular in India. The 'Urdu' used is not a barrier to understanding in India, where many people know Hindi and can easily follow the Urdu spoken.
>
> Today, people prefer to use the terms 'Hindi' or 'Urdu'. The use of the term 'Hindustani' has almost disappeared.

The history of Hindi-Urdu is also complicated because there are a number of other languages spoken in what is today known as the 'Hindi heartland', that stretches from Rajasthan in the west to Bihar and Jharkhand in the east, and from Himachal Pradesh in the north to Chhattisgarh in central India. All these languages are also included in the family of Hindi. Languages like Marwari, Pahari, Braj, Awadhi, Bhojpuri, Maithili, Bundeli, Chhattisgarhi and many others are all considered part of the Hindi universe and their individual histories are all considered as part of the history of Hindi. The 'Hindi' literature of the medieval period was largely in languages like Awadhi, Braj and other languages, not in the Hindi as we understand it today. Modern Hindi literature developed only in the nineteenth century and flourished in the early twentieth century.

Urdu, as a language, developed during the medieval period and the writings of this time, although they are all in the Perso-Arabic script, are somewhat closer to the way we understand Hindi today. But for a number of reasons, Hindi and Urdu, as we shall see, have imagined their history very differently.

THE BEGINNINGS

Hindi, as we know it, evolved from Sanskrit and Shauraseni Prakrit and Apabhramsa.

Prithviraj Raso, written by Chand Bardai (1149–1200?) is considered among the earliest writings in what is today known as Hindi. Chand was the court poet of Prithviraj Chauhan (1166–92/93), who was displaced as ruler of Delhi by Muhammad Ghori (1144–1206). Qutbuddin Aibak succeeded Muhammad Ghori and established the Delhi Sultanate. Over the next six hundred years, except for brief periods, Delhi was ruled by Muslim monarchs, belonging to various dynasties. The last of these dynasties was the Mughals who controlled Delhi and much of north India from 1526 onwards till around 1707. After 1707, with the death of emperor Aurangzeb, the Mughal empire began to shrink as independent rulers, many of whom had been governors under the Mughals, took charge in different parts of the Mughal empire.

It was during these centuries that Hindi-Urdu developed. The language of the region, which had earlier been based on Sanskrit and Prakrit, interacted with the Persian, Turkish and Arabic languages that the Muslim rulers introduced. Through this interaction, Hindi-Urdu developed, largely in Delhi and the regions surrounding it. Hindi-Urdu was also widely used in some of the important cities of northern India, such as Lucknow and Jaunpur. With the expansion of the Delhi Sultanate to the Deccan, Hindi-Urdu spread to those regions, where the language had its own trajectory of development.

DAKHANI

Dakhani is the language of the Deccan, a version of Urdu-Hindi spoken across peninsular India—Maharashtra, Karnataka, Telangana, Andhra Pradesh, Tamil Nadu and in small pockets in Kerala. While Urdu and Hindi form the base of the vocabulary of this language, it has also borrowed words from local languages. In Telangana and Andhra, it borrows Telugu words; in Karnataka, Kannada words; in Maharashtra from Marathi, and so on. It is the first language of many (not all) Muslims in the Deccan region and co-exists with standard Hindi-Urdu as well as the other languages of the region.

Some scholars believe that the language came to the Deccan with Malik Kafur's Deccan military campaigns (1308–11). Others believe a more substantial influence was when Muhammad bin Tughlaq moved the capital to Daulatabad (in modern-day Maharashtra) in 1327 and ordered the people of Delhi to move to the new capital. As a result of these and other events, a population that spoke a northern tongue began to live in the Deccan. Even though Tughlaq later moved the capital back to Delhi in 1335, the language remained. In time, it interacted with the other languages of the region and began to change. Over the next few centuries, Dakhani, as this tongue came to be called, began evolving independently from its northern counterpart.

The famous comedian, Mehmood, first brought this tongue to national notice in the mid-1960s in movies like *Gumnaam*.

Dakhani is a unique amalgam of northern and southern flavours, and a truly representative product of the subcontinent's linguistic diversity.

Hindi-Urdu was far from being the predominant language of northern India. Several other languages, also evolved from Sanskrit and Prakrit, continued to remain in use. The influence of Persian and Turkish was not as great on these languages, as it was on Hindi-Urdu. Languages like Awadhi, Bhojpuri, Maithili, Marwari, Bundeli, Braj and others developed a huge body of literature during the medieval period. Writers like Tulsidas, Kabir, Surdas, Mirabai and many others wrote in these languages. While today, all of them are considered 'Hindi' writers, strictly speaking, the languages they wrote in were somewhat different from Hindi. Why they are considered part of the Hindi language today is something we will understand later.

HINDI-URDU FROM THE NINETEENTH CENTURY TILL INDEPENDENCE

In the later part of Mughal rule, especially in the late eighteenth century, the word 'Urdu' was commonplace to refer to the language spoken in the Mughal court at Delhi, and in the city of Delhi itself and its surrounding areas.

Scholars say that the poet Ghulam Hamadani Mushafi (1750–1824) was among the first to use this term. Prior to this, the poet, Amir Khusrau (1253–1325) had called the language of Delhi, 'Hindavi' or 'Hindi'. 'Dehlavi' and 'Rekhta' had also been used by some writers to refer to this language.

The word 'Urdu' is Turkish in origin and refers to a camp, a military cantonment, or a place of the residence of the elite (*Urdu-e-Mualla*). The courtly Urdu used for poetry and administration consisted of a number of Persian-origin words (and a lesser number of Arabic and Turkish-origin words), though its grammar rules and sentence structure clearly demonstrated its Sanskritic influence. The Urdu of the streets was really 'Hindustani', and it was this tongue that was spoken by the majority of the people in and around Delhi.

But a series of events took place over the course of the nineteenth and early twentieth centuries which resulted in the development of Hindi and Urdu, in the way we understand them today.

After the Battle of Plassey in 1757, the British East India Company established control over Bengal. The British then began to expand their control to large parts of northern and eastern India. To enable proper administration, in 1800, Fort William College was established in Calcutta as a training establishment for officers of the East India Company. An Englishman, John Gilchrist was appointed professor of Hindustani. It was here that Gilchrist, along with Lallooji Lal, another scholar at Fort William, came up with the idea that before northern India came under Muslim rule, a language that was full of Sanskritic words must have existed and that was the 'original' language. But due to the long spell of Muslim rule in north India, that language had been replaced with the Hindustani, that contained many Persian words and that he now heard in the bazaars of north India. This created the basis for 'Hindi', as we understand it today—a language shorn largely of Persian words and consisting of only words of Sanskritic origin. History did not really support this theory, but at that time, the history of Hindi wasn't yet fully explored. Hence, this speculative theory of 'pure' Hindi was not disputed.

> To assess the influence of Sanskrit on Indian languages, one must understand the concept of 'Tatsam' and 'Tadbhav' words. Tatsam are original Sanskrit words which are used in Hindi and other languages in largely unchanged forms. Often, Tatsam words are used more in the written form. Tadbhav words are also derived from Sanskrit but are used in a somewhat altered form clearly different from the original Sanskrit one. For example, the Hindi word, 'pancchi', meaning bird, is a Tadbhav word, which comes from 'pakshi', the original Sanskrit word, which is also sometimes used.

During the nineteenth century, Hindustani consciously transformed itself into 'Hindi' and 'Urdu'. The difference lay largely in vocabulary, with Hindi reaching towards Sanskrit and Urdu reaching towards Persian. The Serampore Press was another important influence in this process. They established publishing houses throughout north India to publish Christian religious literature directed at Hindus and Muslims. They used a Sanskritized language and the Nagari script for literature targeting

Hindus and a Persianized language and the Perso-Arabic script for Muslims.

Along with the development of a separate 'Hindi' and 'Urdu', advocates of both languages became a little more particular about the script, with Hindi preferring the Nagari script (later called Devanagari)[35] and Urdu strictly opting for the Perso-Arabic. These advocates emerged due to a decision made by the East India Company, who by the early nineteenth century controlled most parts of India. In the 1830s, the East India Company administration decided that they would use local languages for administrative purposes and replace the Persian that was then in use. Persian was the language of the Mughal court and the East India Company had for some time continued to use it. But it was decided that this practice needed to change. In the areas surrounding Bombay (Mumbai) and Madras (Chennai), it was easy to make this decision. Marathi and Tamil were the languages used. There was no ambiguity regarding the script either. But in northern India, this was a difficult decision. The choice of the script would effectively decide which language it would be perceived as. The use of the Nagari script would mean 'Hindi' and the use of the Perso-Arabic script would mean 'Urdu'.

During this time, the languages also came to be identified with religions—Hindi came to be regarded as a Hindu language and Urdu as a Muslim one. There were exceptions to this rule, of course, but this was largely the case.

---

[35] Nagari was renamed Deva'nagari—the script of the gods—to give moral authority to Sanskrit. This nomenclature change was deliberate.

> The other script that was also used for writing Hindi was Kaithi. The Kaithi script was closely associated with the Kayasthas, the caste of scribes and record-keepers in the royal courts of northern India. The Kayasthas, although largely Hindu, preferred Urdu. In fact, in the Persian schools of the nineteenth century, Kayastha students were second only to Muslim students. For their own caste-related matters like horoscopes and genealogies, they preferred Kaithi to the Nagari script.

Both Hindi and Urdu now jostled for status under the British administration. Urdu's status weakened considerably after 1857, when Mughal rule in Delhi came to an end. In the meantime, journalist, novelist and religious reformist Bharatendu Harishchandra (1850–85), along with other Hindi proponents, consciously developed literature in Hindi written in the Devanagari script. It was an attempt to be different from Urdu and to develop a language that would stand independently of Urdu. By the early twentieth century, this had more or less come to pass.

In 1900, the Devanagari script was given official status by the British in the region that is now Uttar Pradesh (then called United Provinces which also included today's Uttarakhand). In Bihar and in the Central Provinces (Madhya Pradesh), this had already been done a few years earlier. The Urdu script (therefore Urdu language) already had official status, but now Devanagari (and therefore Hindi) joined it. This proved to be a big boost for Hindi. A number of writings in Hindi had already firmly established the language and the script had also been standardized. The writers of Hindi literature now more consciously

VOWELS

अ आ इ ई उ ऊ ऋ
ए ऐ ओ औ अं अः

CONSONANTS

क ख ग घ ङ
च छ ज झ ञ
ट ठ ड ढ ण
त थ द ध न
प फ ब भ म
य र ल व श ष
स ह क्ष त्र ज्ञ

The Devanagari script

identified with languages like Braj, Awadhi, Bhojpuri and others as its historical progenitors. The Urdu writings of the medieval period were no longer considered part of Hindi's history.

The Urdu script

Meanwhile, Urdu too had become a little more rooted in its milieu. It too developed its own literary history, choosing to identify works written in the Perso-Arabic script as its progenitors, identifying more closely with Persian than it had previously and disregarding the common ground it had with Hindi. Both the languages which had been fellow travellers for centuries now went separate ways.

One person who attempted to bridge the widening chasm between both languages was Mahatma Gandhi. He repeatedly batted for 'Hindi' as the national language.

But Gandhi's Hindi, as he stated in an address to the Hindi Sahitya Sammelan in 1918, included Urdu and as he expressed in his work, *Hind Swaraj*, could be written in either Devanagari or the Persian-derived script. From 1942 onwards, Gandhi chose to use the term 'Hindustani' rather than Hindi, since Hindi by then had come to mean a Sanskritized tongue while Urdu was seen as a Persianized tongue. Gandhi preferred a midpoint that incorporated elements of both—this, in his view, was the language of the common man throughout north India.

Gandhi's influence ensured that the idea of Hindustani continued to stay alive for some more time. After 1947, when the Constitution was being drafted, Nehru and a few others proposed making Hindustani in both scripts the national or official language, but Hindi supporters ensured that this did not happen, and Hindi in the Devanagari script was eventually added.

POST-1947 DILEMMAS

The journey of Hindi-Urdu since 1947 has been a complicated one. The use has increased and while in general, they have become more known and understood, they have also been the target of resentment and hate campaigns by other language-speakers. That is largely because politics around the languages and their use by governments, both in India and in Pakistan, has put an unnatural burden on them. Both are not just languages anymore; they have become vehicles of nationalism.

In India, after 1947, the central government attempted to make Hindi the national language. The belief was that

India needed to do away with colonial influences, and one way to do that was by replacing English with an Indian language. Hindi, its proponents reasoned, was the mother tongue of about forty per cent of the population and hence was the strongest candidate to be declared the national language. But this move was resisted by non-Hindi speakers, who after all constituted sixty per cent of the population. They believed that giving Hindi so much importance would disadvantage the majority of the population whose mother tongue was not Hindi. They reasoned that English needed to continue and the issue of a national language ought to be postponed till a consensus was developed.

When the Constitution came into force in January 1950, Hindi was declared an 'official' language and English an 'associate official' language. Fourteen other languages were declared 'scheduled languages' (this list has now been expanded to twenty-two). It was also decided to continue the use of English for a fifteen-year period, after which it would be entirely replaced with Hindi.

In January 1965, as the date for this switchover loomed large, trouble began brewing in Tamil Nadu. There was considerable resistance to the move to replace English. Protest demonstrations were held and due to the mismanagement of and insensitivity by the administration, some people even ended up sacrificing their lives for the cause of Tamil. Eventually, the central government relented and decided to continue with the use of English as an official language. While this is the current practice, the issue of 'Hindi imposition' does come up from time to time.

When Pakistan was created in 1947, it consisted of two parts: East Pakistan, which was largely Bangla-speaking (who were the majority in the entire country—about forty-two million out of seventy-five million) and West Pakistan, where Punjabi, Sindhi, Pashto, Baloch, Brahui and some other languages were spoken. In the Punjab province, Urdu had been the official language since British times. Urdu was also the language of most of the Muslim migrants from India, who had decided to settle in the newly founded nation. The Pakistani government decided to make Urdu the national language of Pakistan. This move was greatly resented particularly by East Pakistanis, who demanded that Bangla be given equal importance and recognition.

On 21 February 1952, at a protest demonstration for Bangla language rights in Dhaka University, five people were killed when the police opened fire. Over the next two decades, East and West Pakistan clashed repeatedly over language and other issues. In 1971, the resentment boiled over and the nation split, with East Pakistanis choosing to constitute a separate nation—Bangladesh (the land of Bangla). The issue of language was resolved through separation.

Since 1999, 21 February has been observed as International Mother Language Day the world over. This is a tribute to the language movement in East Pakistan (now Bangladesh) and in memory of the five people killed for language rights. Bangladeshis observe this day as one of tragedy and mourning. The Ekushey Book Fair is held in the month of February in remembrance of this time (Ekushey is Bangla for 'twenty-first').

THE LANGUAGES TODAY

Hindi, today, is probably more widely used than it has ever been through its entire history. It is the official language of several states in India and the popularity of Hindi films (more correctly, Hindustani films) has ensured that the language is understood over almost the entire country and in many other parts of the world too. Hindi literature is also extremely dynamic and popular.

There are now variants of Hindi. 'Bambaiyya', the Hindi spoken in Mumbai, is one such variant. A Hindi-English combination ('Hinglish') is also a popularly used tongue. Hindi has also found unusual homes. In Arunachal Pradesh, it is Hindi that has become the lingua franca among the various tribes of the region.

Hindi is also spoken in many other parts of the world, wherever Indian migrants migrated in the nineteenth century. From Surinam in South America to Mauritius near Africa to Trinidad in the West Indian islands and Fiji near Australia, Hindi or languages similar to it are spoken.

In Surinam in South America, a language called Sarnami is spoken by people of Indian origin who live there. Sometimes called Surinam Hindustani, it is a mixture of the Indian tongues like Awadhi, Bhojpuri and the other languages of north India that the early immigrants from India to Surinam spoke. It has also adopted words from Dutch (Surinam was a Dutch colony) and Sranan Tongo (a local language). The Indian community in Surinam is 1.25 lakh strong and continues to use the language today.

Similarly, Urdu has become the lingua franca of Pakistan and found wide acceptance. It continues to be in use in India too and is one of the twenty-two scheduled languages.

Hindi and Urdu literature are also extremely popular. Their sheer range has ensured that there is something to cater to all tastes. From highbrow literature and poetry to pulp fiction, from serious drama that incorporates the best of European and Indian tradition to drama that caters to the popular taste, the literatures have it all.

In Hindi, writers like Munshi Premchand (who also wrote in Urdu), Nirmal Verma, Jaishankar Prasad, Mahadevi Verma, Kamleshwar, Jainendra, Mohan Rakesh, Harishankar Parsai, Krishna Sobti and many others are hugely popular. In 2022, Geetanjali Shree's *Tomb of Sand* (originally published in Hindi as *Ret Samadhi* and translated into English by Daisy Rockwell) won the Booker Prize.

In Urdu, the writings of Mirza Ghalib, Mir Taqi Mir, Saadat Hasan Manto, Ismat Chughtai, Faiz Ahmed Faiz, Krishan Chander, Rajinder Singh Bedi, Qurratulain Hyder and many others are extremely popular.

There continues to be resistance to Hindi imposition in India and to Urdu imposition in Pakistan. Equally, the usage of these languages is also growing. How the governments handle the matter of these two languages from an official standpoint will determine their future destiny and trajectory.

TIMELINE

1150–1200: Chand Bardai writes *Prithviraj Raso*.

1206: Establishment of the Delhi Sultanate.

Around 1300: Amir Khusrau uses the term 'Hindavi' to refer to the language of Delhi.

Around 1775–1800: Ghulam Hamadani Mushafi uses the term 'Urdu'.

1800s and early 1900s: Hindustani develops into 'Hindi' and 'Urdu'.

1947: Urdu is declared the national language of Pakistan.

1950: Hindi is declared an 'official language' of India.

1966: Anti-Hindi protests in Tamil Nadu.

Together, about 831 million speakers speak Hindi-Urdu as their first or second language.[36]

---

[36] James Lane, 'The Ten Most Spoken Languages in the World', 9 February 2023, https://www.babbel.com/en/magazine/the-10-most-spoken-languages-in-the-world

THE STORY OF BRAHMI

In 1837, an ancient mystery was finally solved. In a research paper verbosely titled 'Interpretation of the most ancient of the inscriptions on the pillar called the lat of Feroz Shah, near Delhi, and of the Allahabad, Radhia and Mattiah pillar, or lat, inscriptions which agree therewith', James Prinsep, founding editor of the *Journal of the Asiatic Society of Bengal* and assay master[37] of the Benares and Calcutta mints, announced his decoding of the Brahmi script.

A reward for this decoding had been on offer since 1354. In that year, Feroz Shah Tughlaq brought an iron pillar from Ambala to Ferozabad, the new city that he was founding near Delhi. Tughlaq offered a reward to anyone who could read the mysterious writing on the pillar, but nobody could.

Norwegian Christian Lassen had in 1836 deciphered some Brahmi letters. But it was Prinsep who decoded the script completely. Prinsep's efforts were aided by Pali texts from Sri Lanka. In the next couple of years, Prinsep

---

[37] An officer who assays or tests the purity of the gold or silver coins.

was able to connect the inscriptions on the pillar to the Mauryan emperor, Ashoka (reigned 268–231 BCE).

In the next few years, many Ashokan rock edicts, almost all written in the Prakrit language and the Brahmi script (a small number were in the Kharoshthi script, mostly found in present-day Pakistan) were read and the history of that period could now be reconstructed better than it could be earlier.

ORIGINS OF THE SCRIPT

Almost all the earliest available examples of Brahmi script are from inscriptions from the times of emperor Ashoka. The only evidence of writing in the Indian subcontinent older than Brahmi is the script of the Indus Valley civilization, which has not yet been deciphered and which does not seem to have any connection to the Brahmi script.

But when and how did the Brahmi script originate?

Georg Bühler, the German Indologist, protégé of Max Muller and author of *On the Origin of the Indian Brahma Alphabet* (1898), believes that the Brahmi script originates from the Northern Semitic or Phoenician script from western Asia. His judgment is based on the similarities of some of the letters. This hasn't been fully accepted by scholars.

Other scholars think that the script probably did not develop from an earlier script and was actually an invention based on the orders of a Mauryan emperor, possibly Chandragupta Maurya or even Ashoka himself. To create this script, the theory goes, the older Kharosthi

Ashokan Brahmi (vowels and consonants)

script, mostly written from right to left, may have served as a model though Brahmi itself was written from left to right. Kharosthi originated due to the influence of the Semitic script used by the Persians. It was originally used to write Gandhari Prakrit.

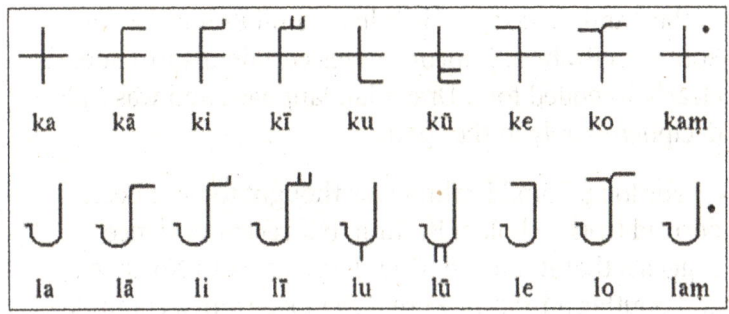

Ashokan Brahmi (consonants with the vowel sounds)

There is some evidence to support the invention theory. Megasthenes, who visited the court of Chandragupta Maurya (somewhere between 305 to 281 BCE), observed that there was no prevalent writing system. This implies that the script was developed later, perhaps for administrative reasons. The Mauryan empire was vast and governing this large and diverse territory would have been difficult without a script to pass on instructions to its various officials.

Initially, Brahmi was referred to as the 'pin-man' script or the 'stick figure' script, because of the appearance of its letters. Georg Bühler called the script 'Brahma' in the nineteenth century. But the name 'Brahmi' stuck after scholars associated the pin-man script with the Brahmi script mentioned in the list of scripts in the *Lalitavistara Sūtra*, a Buddhist text from the third century CE. Interestingly, the *Lalitavistara Sutra* mentions sixty-four scripts, among them the Dravida script, which is perhaps a reference to a script used in the southern part of the Indian subcontinent.

This southern script, a variation of Ashokan or Northern Brahmi, has been discovered in inscriptions in the Tamil region and is called Tamil Brahmi or Southern Brahmi. It incorporates certain distinct sounds clearly intended for a Dravidian language and was fully deciphered only in the 1950s.

For long, Tamil Brahmi was thought to have been derived from Ashokan Brahmi, but recent evidence suggests that it may be older. Perhaps, both Northern and Southern Brahmi were developed from a common source which is as yet unknown. But what is clear is that both scripts are related. Later, they evolved independently to develop into various other scripts, the descendants of which are widely used today.

INFLUENCE

A later, more refined version of the Brahmi script called Gupta Brahmi was widely used between the fourth and sixth centuries CE at the time of the Gupta dynasty. The Allahabad inscription, which Prinsep mentions in the title of his research paper, is an example of Gupta Brahmi, but the language of that inscription is Sanskrit, unlike the Ashokan inscription on the same pillar, which is in Prakrit.

The Gupta Brahmi script evolved into three separate scripts: Nagari, Sharda and Siddham. The Nagari script later evolved into Devanagari, the present-day script of Hindi, Nepali, Marathi and Dogri. A variant of Devanagari is used to write Gujarati as well. Besides Devanagari, the Nandinagari and Kaithi scripts too are derived from the original Nagari. Nandinagari was for long used to write Sanskrit in southern India. Kaithi or Kayastha was at one time widely used and was a close competitor to Devanagari

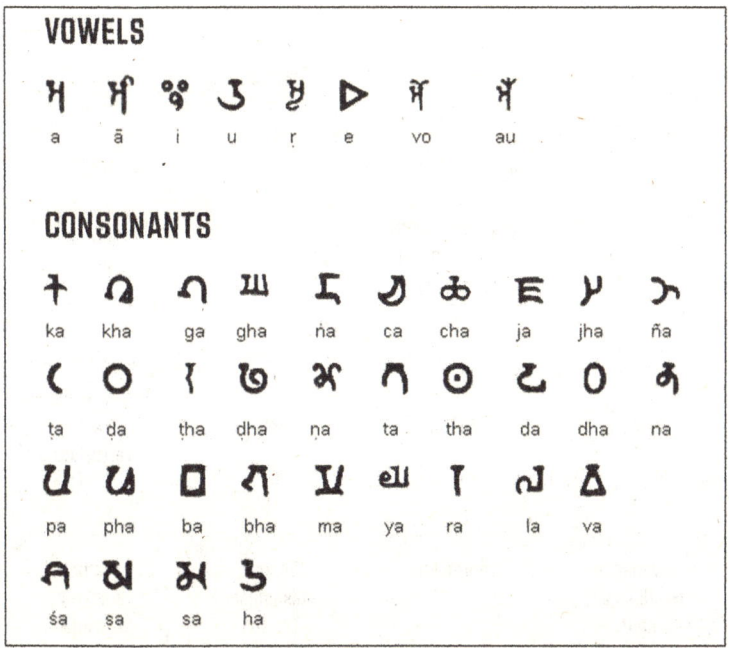

VOWELS

| a | ā | i | u | ṛ | e | vo | au |

CONSONANTS

ka	kha	ga	gha	ṅa	ca	cha	ja	jha	ña
ṭa	ḍa	ṭha	ḍha	ṇa	ta	tha	da	dha	na
pa	pha	ba	bha	ma	ya	ra	la	va
śa	ṣa	sa	ha

Gupta Brahmi

to write Hindi, even in the early twentieth century. But now it has almost vanished.

The Sharda script influenced Gurumukhi, the script used to write Punjabi in Indian Punjab (Pakistani Punjab uses the Shahmukhi script) and also survives in old documents and manuscripts of the Kashmiri Pandit community. The Siddham script eventually gave rise to the Bangla, Assamese, Tibetan and the old Maithili scripts (Maithili is mostly written in Devanagari now).

Besides the script, the organization of the Brahmi alphabet in terms of sounds also had a wide-ranging influence. In *Languages and Nations: The Dravidian Proof in Colonial Madras* (2006), Thomas Trautman talks of how

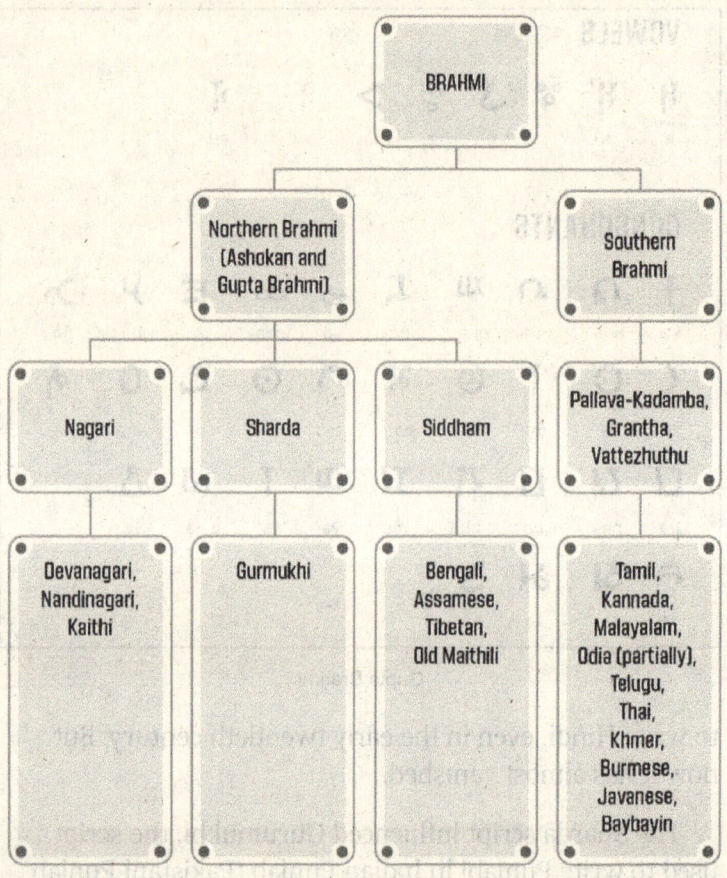

it is likely that it indirectly influenced the Japanese kana and Korean writing systems.

Southern Brahmi later evolved into the Pallava-Kadamba script and also into the Grantha and Vattezuthu scripts. Grantha, Vattezhuthu and the Kadamba script eventually evolved into the modern-day writing systems of Tamil, Kannada, Telugu and Malayalam. It also influenced the Odia script (Odia was also greatly influenced by Bangla).

Besides these, the present-day Sinhalese, Thai, Khmer and Burmese scripts too owe their origin to the Southern Brahmi script. The now extinct Javanese system of Indonesia is also a descendant of Southern Brahmi. The Baybayin script system of the Philippines has also clearly developed from Southern Brahmi.

From modern-day Punjab and Kashmir to southeast Asia and even beyond, Brahmi's influence is visible to this day.

THE STORY OF HINGLISH

Hinglish is something most of us would have noticed. It is used in advertising jingles and Bollywood movie titles. This strengthens the impression that it is a recent phenomenon.

But it is actually a couple of centuries old. In 1827, Henry Louis Vivian Derozio (1809–31), India's first English poet, in his poem 'Ode—From the Persian of Half' Queez' wrote:

Without thy dreams, dear opium,
Without a single hope I am,
Spicy scent, delusive joy;
Chillum hither lao, my boy!

This was a sprinkling of Hindi in an English poem.

In 1887, Ayodhya Prasad Khatri (1857–1905), did the reverse—sprinkled English in Hindi in these lines about life under British rule:

Rent Law *ka gham karen ya* Bill of Income Tax *ka*?
Kya karen apna nahin hai sense right now-a-days.

Darkness *chhaaya hua hai Hind mein chaaro taraf*
Naam ki bhi hai nahin baaqi na light now-a-days.

So, what is Hinglish, really? Is it English with a sprinkling
of Hindi words like what Derozio did? Or is it Hindi with
a few English words or phrases thrown in, in the manner
of Khatri? Also, is it only this hybrid of English and Hindi
that needs to be looked at closely? What about the fact that
English has also made its way into the other languages
of India and that other hybrids have emerged as a result:
Tanglish (Tamil and English), Kanglish (Kannada and
English), Bonglish/Benglish (Bangla and English), Punglish
(Punjabi and English) and so on. All of these are similar to
the Hinglish phenomenon. So perhaps the correct name
for these tongues should be 'Inglish'.

Linguists call this phenomenon of multi-lingual
speakers alternating between two or more languages
during a single conversation, 'code-switching' or 'code-
mixing'. Code-switching is different from 'borrowing'
when a word from one language is borrowed and used in
another without translation. A good example of this are
the words, 'kindergarten' (German for children's garden),
'bazaar' (Persian for market) and 'ballet' (from French).
Code-mixing goes beyond borrowing. It is to actually
think and articulate in two or more languages to make
oneself clearly understood. This *khichdi* of English and a
local language is not an exclusively Indian phenomenon,
though. Other such tongues exist: Spanglish (Spanish and
English) has been observed in many parts of the US, and
Taglish (Tagalog and English) is spoken in the Philippines.

It is difficult to say when Inglish became a widely
used tongue. But it is perhaps easier to identify how

and why English invaded Indian language spaces. After Independence, some politicians tried to make Hindi the 'national language'. This failed due to resistance from non-Hindi speakers and also because English was the language of higher education, law and trade. For a time, English and Hindi were in competition, with Hindi clearly ruling the heart, at least of some (Hindi films became popular nationally during this time) and English the head (as the language of education and 'sophistication'). In time, knowing English became almost a necessity and it has become a symbol of modernity and aspiration. But forsaking Hindi (or local languages) is not an option either. Hinglish and Inglish therefore help bridge this gap.

More than anything else, Inglish is perhaps proof that English is now an Indian tongue and has found comfort and acceptance.

FURTHER READING

1. *Languages of India* by Gopal Haldar, translated by Tista Bagchi (National Book Trust India, 2000)

2. *Hindi Nationalism* by Alok Rai (Sangam Books, 2001)

3. *Text and Tradition in South India* by Velcheru Narayana Rao (The Orient Blackswan, 2016)

4. *Tamil: A Biography* by David Shulman (Harvard University Press, 2016)

5. *Mother Tongue: The English Language* by Bill Bryson (William Morrow Paperbacks, 2001)

6. *The English Language: A Guided Tour of the Language* by David Crystal (Penguin Books, 2002)

7. *The Adventure of English: The Biography of a Language* by Melvyn Bragg (Hodder & Stoughton, 2004)

8. *Modern Linguistics: The Results of Chomsky's Revolution* by Neil Smith and Deirdre Wilson (Penguin Books, 1991)

9. *Wanderers, Kings, Merchants: The Story of India Through Its Languages* by Peggy Mohan (Penguin Random House India, 2021)

10. *Through the Language Glass: Why The World Looks Different In Other Languages* by Guy Deutscher (Random House, 2016)

THANKS

To Amarinder, for everything.

To Sayoni Basu, old friend and editor, whose idea the book was.

To Gayatri, sister, supporter and rock. To Amma and Appa, for love.

To Geet and Neil, for the fun times. To Nethra, for even more fun times.

To Norah for company.

To Preeti, Venu, Sanghamitra, Deepthi, Arundathi, Amandeep, Lakshmi, for friendship and belief.

To Sanjay D'Souza for banter.

Karthik Venkatesh grew up in Bangalore, speaking Tamil, Malayalam, Kannada, English, Dakhani and Hindi. He tried to learn French but failed. He did learn Punjabi though.

Once an MBA, he later studied education and taught English and History in a school. He now edits for a living and writes whenever the fancy strikes him.

Karthik lives in Bangalore with his wife Amarinder, children Geet and Neil, and dog Norah. He has plans to adopt another dog and have a mini aquarium. On weekday mornings, he often runs. On weekends, he naps.

Read more in the series

10 INDIAN MONARCHS WHOSE AMAZING STORIES YOU MAY NOT KNOW

Devika Rangachari

This book tells the stories of ten Indian monarchs who find, at best, passing mention in the history textbooks we read, though their lives were exciting and their achievements considerable:

Ajatashatru	Didda
Bindusara	Ramapala
Rudradaman	Abbakka
Pulakeshin II	Chand Bibi
Jayapida	Ahilyabai Holkar

Historian and award-winning novelist, Devika Rangachari writes absorbing tales of the men and women who shaped lives and kingdoms in their times.

Read more in the series

10 INDIAN ART MYSTERIES THAT HAVE NEVER BEEN SOLVED

Mamta Nainy

This book tells the stories of ten mysterious people, styles and objects in Indian art from the prehistoric period to the present day-and in the process, it captures some of the diversity and range of the very large canvas we call Indian art. The stories told here include those of:

The Bhimbetka paintings

The evolution of the Buddha

The Ajanta caves

The Kailashanatha temple

The Pithora paintings

Women artists of the Mughal era

Bani Thani

Indian yellow

Manaku of Guler

The Sripuranthan Shiva Nataraja

Mamta Nainy explores diverse artistic periods, explains different art forms, and gives insights into the lives of artists working in different times and spaces, one curious case at a time.